RIDING THE SHORTWAVES:

Exploring the Magic of Amateur Radio

By Don Keith N4KC

Also by Don Keith

The Forever Season
Wizard of the Wind
The Rolling Thunder Stockcar Racing Series (with Kent Wright)
Final Bearing (with George Wallace)
Gallant Lady (with Ken Henry)
In the Course of Duty
The Bear: the Legendary Life of Coach Paul "Bear" Bryant
Final Patrol
The Ice Diaries (with Captain William R. Anderson)
War Beneath the Waves
We Be Big (with Rick Burgess and Bill "Bubba" Bussey KJ4JJ)
Undersea Warrior
Firing Point (with George Wallace)

Writing as Jeffery Addison with Edie Hand:

The Last Christmas Ride
The Soldier's Ride
The Christmas Ride: the Miracle of the Lights

www.donkeith.com   www.n4kc.com

© 2012 by Don Keith

All rights reserved. No portion of this work may be reproduced without express permission of the author except for brief excerpts in reviews. Please contact the author for permission to reproduce any portion of this book in such publications as amateur radio club newsletters or ham radio-oriented periodicals.

Some of the material in this book has appeared in varying forms—with permission—on web sites and in other publications.

TABLE OF CONTENTS

Introduction: the Magic is Still There...on the Shortwaves 6

Chapter 1 -- Someday..17

Chapter 2 -- Caveat Emptor: Thoughts While Perusing a Ham Radio Catalog 37

Chapter 3 -- Reading Between the Lines 43

Chapter 4 -- A Short Guided Tour of the Amateur Radio Shortwave Bands 49

Chapter 5 -- The Amazing Disappearing Antenna 74

Chapter 6 -- The Top Five "Get on the Air Quickly" Antennas 91

Chapter 7 -- Lessons from the Old Timers 114

Chapter 8 -- The Antenna Party..133

Chapter 9 -- Resonance Schmesonance! 150

Chapter 10 -- Feeding the Beast—Transferring Radio Frequency Energy from Your Transmitter to Your Antenna 158

Chapter 11 -- What? You Only Have ONE Antenna? 174

Chapter 12 -- Ten Reasons You Should Learn Dah – di – dah – dit Di – dah - dah 182

Chapter 13 -- The SOS Trail 192

Chapter 14 -- I See Your Lips Moving, but… 207

Chapter 15 -- Why it is Easier than Ever for You to Talk to the World 217

Chapter 16 -- The One-Hundred-Country Wager 228

Chapter 17 -- Everybody's S-Meter is Correct!...252

Chapter 18 -- A Dark and Stormy Night..262

Chapter 19 -- You might be a "REAL HAM" if… 276

Chapter 20 -- What Have You Done for Me Lately? 281

Chapter 21 -- The Saddest Words I Know 295

Chapter 22 -- Amateur Radio is Not for Everybody: a Primer for the Ham Evangelist 303

Chapter 23 -- My Top Ten Suggestions for Newly Licensed Amateurs 314

Chapter 24 -- The Roundtable 330

Introduction: the Magic is Still There...on the Shortwaves

Even though we amateur radio enthusiasts consider ourselves to be communicators, it is really difficult sometimes for us to convey to other folks exactly what it is that makes our hobby so special to us. What makes it so addictive and fulfilling, so magnetic. Personally, I have been in and out of the hobby for over fifty years now, yet I find its allure to be just as strong now as it was way back when the bug first bit me. And let me assure you, it bit me hard!

That was when I heard those first squeaks and squawks of Morse code, the dits and dahs of those characters riding in on the wind as they formed my call letters. The exciting, exclusive call sign that had been newly-assigned to me by that awe-inducing agency, the Federal Communications Commission. There they were, those letters with the number "4" in the middle that quickly became so much a part of who I was. And despite my nervousness at the outset of that first conversation on the air (a "QSO"), I immediately recognized *my* call sign ringing back at me out of a receiver tuned to the shortwaves.

That exhilarating reply came in response to a "CQ"—a blind call into the ether—looking for someone—anyone—with whom to chat. And, I must admit, I was half hoping nobody would answer that first time I sent out that blanket request for a contact. The prospects of it all scared me just a little bit.

But when it actually happened, it was nothing short of supernatural!

Now it is true that amateur (or "ham") radio led to a career in broadcasting for me, but I have no doubt I would still love it just as much, even if I had gone a different direction in life. The hobby has helped many people break into and follow careers in communications, electronics, computers, engineering and more. However, many thousands of other hams have different interests and avocations, many decidedly non-technical. You do not have to be a geek to be a ham.

Oh, I admit that there were years when I did not even turn on a rig—what we call our radios—years when job, family, my book-writing and other distractions took me away from the magic I had experienced as a 13-year-old kid, living down on that isolated farm in rural Alabama. But I always came back to the hobby, and I do not exaggerate when I tell you that each return was even sweeter and more electrifying than the last.

Even though amateur radio had changed each time— sometimes dramatically so with new shortwave bands at our disposal, new and exotic modes of communication available to us, different facets of radio, all calling out to me to come give them a try—I still found the basics of it all virtually the same. Those same intangible attractions were still there. And they were still just as difficult to explain to the great unwashed out there. I still feel sorry for those who do not know or care about the radio spectrum and the electromagnetic waves—the magical pixie dust that swirls around all of us out there on the wind.

It is also true that some doubt the value of the hobby today, it being based on such old technology after all. People have smart phones, video games, the Internet, YouTube, and Facebook. Kids who once might have been fascinated by talking to someone across the continent on the ham radio now do it routinely in chat groups, on Facebook, or via texting. Who wants to hang wire and create radio-frequency energy when all this new technology is all around us?

It is true as well that the hobby came into official being, set up by Congress, in 1912, making it over 100 years old.

First, I should point out that there are more amateur radio licensees in the United States today than ever before. We are at an all-time high. The rest of the world has also seen a resurgence in interest in the hobby, including some of its more antiquated technology, such as Morse code.

Still, the questions come.

"Can't you do the same thing on the Internet?"

"I can talk all over the world on my cell phone. I don't need a radio or a tower or all that wire in the sky."

"Why use that Morse stuff when you can just text somebody and tell them what you want to tell them?"

Yes, you can. You can do all those things.

But the people asking those questions are missing the point entirely. It is exasperating to us ham-nuts that they do not seem willing to even try to understand what draws people to amateur radio. And it is vexing to us that we cannot do a better job of explaining the attraction.

It is a mystery to us why they dismiss us, stick their noses against a computer monitor or mobile device and refuse to come join us and experience all the fun we are having. We cannot understand why they do not simply see for themselves what the hobby is really all about and why we love it so. Though it is not true, we are certain every single one of them would catch the fever just as surely as we all did.

In my frustration, I often fire back in reply to such questions with, "Why do you go fishing? You can buy fish at the grocery store. You're a golfer. Why don't you just walk over and drop the ball into the hole instead of teeing it up and whacking it three or four times—eight or ten whacks at the ball if you are me?

"Tell you what. Take the 'N4KC Challenge.' Pull out that fancy cell phone of yours and dial a number totally at random, using some area code on the other side of the planet. Then see what kind of conversation you will have with whoever answers. If anybody answers.

"Where's the magic? The cell phone works about the same every time you try it. There is no thrill in getting somebody to say, 'Hello.' But the ionosphere changes all the time. When you send out a radio signal on the amateur radio shortwave bands from your own station, you never know for sure where it will bounce back to earth or who will answer your call.

"However, you will know one thing for sure. It takes skill to do what you just did. And the fellow on the other end of that enchanted radio circuit will appreciate the magic of what is happening just as much as you do. You will have common ground. Regardless where you were born, where you live, what kind of government you have, what language you mostly speak, or where you are on the this big blue ball we all inhabit, you and that other person out there in the ether are automatically members of the same tribe."

Usually when I go into that rant, the other people just wave me off and I let it go. But sometimes they nod or chew their lips, or give me some kind of sign that they understand what I am trying to say. Then, when I sense the slightest bit of interest, I plunge ahead with my evangelical message.

"To add to the magic of it all, you may be talking across the country or all the way around the world, to an astronaut in space, to a rock and roll star, to a local guy on the way to the supermarket. You may eavesdrop on emergency communications in the wake of a hurricane, a network of guys devoted to restoring old motorcycles, a man operating from a mountain summit on solar power or from the shadow of an isolated lighthouse, or a missionary in a South American jungle talking back to family or supporters in the USA. No matter what you are doing, you are using a radio station you put together and made work in order to accomplish that miraculous feat. You may have bought the gear—almost certainly did nowadays—and you merely followed the instructions to hook it up and put it on the air. Or you may have soldered the parts onto a circuit board or designed and put up the antenna that is casting those electromagnetic waves off into space. In order to earn your license, you learned enough rules and regulations and basic electronics to pass the test and to put your station on the air. You figured out enough propagation theory to decide on which shortwave band you could most likely conjure up a conversation at a particular time of day. You know enough by that point to put out a clean signal, coax most of the power out of the transmitter and up the feed line to the antenna, and be confident that your signal will be conducted out into space. You acquired enough knowledge to be able to pull a signal out of the atmospheric noise and carry on a conversation using voice, Morse code, the ones-and-zeroes of digital communications, your own television station, or some other mode you have learned about and now understand how and why it works.

"See, there is fulfillment in that. There is self-satisfaction. Accomplishment. There is...well...magic in the air anytime you are riding the shortwaves!"

Despite being a man of words—a former broadcaster and a writer with over two dozen published books to my credit—and having been a passionate amateur radio enthusiast for over half a century, that is about as good a job as I can manage in describing the allure of our hobby to someone who knows little about it.

Maybe the best thing I could say is this: once you catch the fever, you will know it. You will not be able to easily kick it. And you will find it just as difficult as I do to explain it to someone else.

That goes along with being in the "tribe," the "fraternity" (or "sorority") of ham radio.

Oh, some people come into our ranks and then quickly lose interest. That is true with any endeavor. Great as it is, our hobby is not for everybody. That is difficult for many of us hams to believe, but it is true.

However, if it really bites you, you stay bitten. You will be, forevermore, a "ham."

That elusive enchantment is what I have tried to portray in this collection of fictional stories—some of them made up completely, others based on real people or incidents. I have also included some short articles that I hope will be of interest to potential hams, newcomers, or even old-timers. The aim is to help each of them, regardless their experience or interests, to get more out of this wonderful, addictive hobby. Maybe they will get all wild-eyed and zealous, too, just as many of us tend to do when promoting the hobby.

To me, this seems like a good way to evangelize about ham radio in a sneaky sort of way, and to show the fascination our hobby offers in the best manner I know how.

I hope those who have an interest in radio will become inspired by these tales and articles and decide to learn more. I also hope those who, like me, are already active in the hobby, still drawn to its magnetism, will simply enjoy the stories and articles in this book for what they are, one guy's love sonnet to a pastime that has given him so much pleasure, satisfaction and education.

Oh, and maybe some of them will pass this book along to others who might be teetering on the edge. You have my permission to do so. Maybe just this one little shove will be all it takes to push them off the cliff and have them join our growing numbers.

Allow them to experience the satisfaction, learning, and just plain fun this fascinating hobby can provide.

Encourage them to join us out there—*riding on the shortwaves*.

Okay, let's begin with a story that demonstrates all this magic I have been talking about. Or at least the magic discovered one night by a young man named Greg Cooper as he was postponing doing his math homework.

If you are brand new to the hobby, not all the terminology in this story will make sense to you yet. Even some who have been around for a while may not be familiar with the vintage gear our characters use to communicate with and get to know each other. Some of the equipment and background are from the 1960s. But I believe you will get the message.

Many of us found our professions directly as a result of our early interest in amateur radio. You do not have to be a technical whiz, or even technically inclined. But there are many aspects of the hobby that can direct you toward a vocation or make you stronger in the one you choose.

And if you get hooked, I guarantee you will have many, many similar experiences to the ones you will read about here, once you are on the wind.

Now, let us imagine a dark, cold night, in a time before many of you were born...

Chapter 1 -- Someday

The signals from the Japanese stations, now reedy and watery in the frying sizzle of band noise, were struggling to make the long trip over the North Pole. Hams in Europe had long since gone to bed. The Brazilians had given up, too, chucking twenty meters for some other amateur radio band or gone off to pour themselves a late night coffee. Even the usual wall of stations on the East Coast of the U.S.A. had apparently grown tired of the noise and the puny signals and pulled down their shades, too.

Greg Cooper twisted the tuning knob on his Hallicrafters S-38 receiver, swishing it back forth around 14.250 on the twenty-meter phone band. He ignored the noticeable jump in frequency when the knot in the dial string caught on its guide. He had been meaning to re-string it, but school and football and girls kept getting in the way of that chore. It was after ten o'clock so the lights were out in his bedroom, but the warm glow of the 6146 final amplifier tube in the Globe Scout transmitter still gave enough luminance through the holes in the cabinet for him to be able to log a contact.

That is, if he ever was able to make one.

Greg still only had the one crystal from his Novice days, cut for 7.125 in the middle of the forty-meter Novice band. Now that he had upgraded to the General Class license, he could use it on

14.250—the second harmonic and in the AM portion of the band—if he remembered to find the correct dip in the transmitter's final when he tuned it up. He employed the same dipole antenna as he used for 40 meters, too, 63 feet long, fed somewhere near the middle with coax cable. The coil in the output circuit of the Scout sparked and spat at him sometimes when he tuned up on twenty meters, but he got by and had made a smattering of short contacts since upgrading to General. They had all ended with the other station losing him in the static or the omnipresent interference. And every one of them had lost him before he could even get the other stations to understand his name and location.

    Greg shoved the cowlick out of his eyes, glanced at the unopened algebra book on the bed, and gave himself three more minutes to conjure up a QSO (conversation over the air with another amateur radio station) before surrendering to homework. Neither of his parents was a ham radio operator and they had trouble understanding his affection for whooshing static and the squeaking, squawking noises that spilled from the receiver's speaker.

    Homework had to come first, they maintained. Especially math if he ever wanted to become an engineer, as he professed.

    It was getting late. The full moon filtered through the blinds at his window. There was already a hint of frost at the bottom of each windowpane. There would be snow to shovel in no time, and that, too, would carve into his ham radio time.

With a flick of the wrist—just the way he had seen his uncle do it with his much bigger and better ham radio station—Greg ventured away from his rock-bound frequency and checked the rest of the band. There were only weedy snatches of voices, a whistling tease of a Morse code character, and lots of atmospheric scratching. He spun the dial back to the vicinity of 14.250 and reached for the power on/off switch on the transmitter.

Much as he hated to, he had to crack that homework. If there was only some way to become an engineer without dealing with that dang math!

But then he noticed a low rumble in the speaker. He touched the receiver dial, moved a few cycles down, and the rumble became a piercing whine. Somebody was tuning up his transmitter, right there on "his" frequency. Greg squinted at the math book, pursed his lips, and switched the AM/CW switch on the Hallicrafters receiver to AM. With his fingertips, he lightly touched the orange cover of the crystal that protruded from the front of the Scout, as if that would assure he was on frequency and tuned up, ready to transmit should he hear a potential station come on, ready to talk.

No worries. Greg had dipped the plate three times already, whistled into the microphone, and watched the plate current meter swing with his words. The transmitter was as ready as it would ever be. Now if the propagation gods would just cooperate for a few minutes.

The big signal had wiped the band clean, shoving away the static, and as its owner tuned up some more, it got even stronger. Now Greg could hear the sound of someone fiddling with knobs and throwing switches. Then the slight rasp of the operator gently clearing his throat. In the background, there was the soft hum of what must have been a fan, maybe shuttling cool air over some powerful, glowing amplifier tubes.

Greg still pictured the gentle process of tuning up a big ham radio station as something akin to a wizard, mixing his potions, chanting his incantations, casting a spell on something over which mere mortals had no control. That was the way Uncle Max did it. Always in the same order and with an exaggerated flourish, always watching the string of meters across the faces of his transmitter and rack-mounted amplifier. And Max never settled for anything but a perfect tune. If even one meter was off a few milliamps or volts, he fiddled with the knobs and switches some more until everything was plumb.

"This is Zed Dee Eight Alpha Alpha, tuning and standing by."

The deep voice roared out of the speaker, rattling Greg's pencil on the desk. Eyes wide, he grabbed for the "Volume" knob and twisted it counter-clockwise.

Lord! Mom would have his hide if he woke up his father. Dad had to be at the mill at six the next morning. He worked hard and needed his rest.

Without even taking the time to consult the sheet of paper on the wall that listed all the world's amateur radio call signs, Greg flipped the S-38 to "Standby." Then, with a practiced motion, he threw the Scout's switch to "Transmit," even as he grabbed the cheap microphone in the other hand. Sometimes he still got the switching operation backward, and the resulting squeal left him deaf for a moment, more worried about the paper in the cone of the speaker than his eardrums. He would have to borrow a set of cans (headphones) from his uncle if he busted the speaker.

"ZD8AA…ZD8AA," his voice broke on the second "ZD8AA." The guy on the other end would certainly know now that he was only a kid, fourteen years old. Shoot! No real ham wanted to waste time talking to a kid. And especially if the amateur operator he was calling was in some exotic, faraway, foreign land.

Greg swallowed hard and tried to lower his voice again without it cracking this time, struggling to sound at least seventeen.

"This is WA8QJK. WA8QJK in Cleveland, Ohio, calling. Do you copy? Over. "

Nothing.

Nothing but the crackling of static, the distant whine on his receiver from Mr. Oliver's TV set down the block. (Mr. Oliver still fussed about Johnny Carson replacing Jack Paar on "The Tonight Show," but he watched every night anyway.) Greg could even hear a car passing by on the street outside his window, which he had to leave open just enough to allow the coax and the chill wind to get underneath.

Missed another one, he thought. Maybe somebody else would call the fellow and he could postpone the algebra homework a few more minutes while he at least eavesdropped on an honest-to-goodness QSO.

Then the crackle was once again erased by the quieting of the massive signal, rolling in on the ether from wherever it came from. Let's see who he answered him, Greg thought. Hopefully it would be somebody outside Greg's skip zone so he could overhear both sides of the conversation.

"Yes, good morning from Ascension Island in the South Pacific, where it *is*, by the way, already morning. WA8QJK, this is ZD8AA. You're not real strong but I think I will be able to pull you out of the mud. I'll call it four-by-five. My name is Steve. Sierra tango echo victor echo. Steve. And I am on Ascension, an island between South America and the west coast of the continent of Africa. Pretty isolated territory, but the weather is nice most of the time. I appreciate you giving me a report on how you are hearing 'Ole Betsy' tonight. So, how copy, Old Man? WA8QJK from ZD8AA. Over."

Greg did not even have time to worry about his voice breaking this time, to appreciate the irony of this operator calling him an "Old Man." All hams called each other "Old Man," or just "OM."

He toggled the switches on his receiver and transmitter—in the correct order, twice in a row, a new record!—and put his lips to the microphone.

Like a true old-timer, Greg Cooper gave Steve on Ascension Island an "honest-to-goodness" five-by-nine for a signal report. He told him his name and location, and just a bit about his simple station, the Hallicrafters, the Globe Scout, the forty-meter dipole zigzagging among the big elms in their tiny backyard. Before he realized it, Greg had talked a full three minutes. He had never transmitted for three full minutes in his entire amateur radio career. His year-and-a-half amateur radio career.

Oh, no. ZD8AA would certainly have lost him in the underbrush by now. Greg's frail little signal had surely been swallowed up by the atmosphere and the thousands of miles between him and that island out there between South America and the west coast of Africa. Maybe, if so, he would pull the J-38 key over and try to rekindle the contact on CW (Morse code). He was not about to give up easily on this one.

But the instant he took the receiver off standby, he heard the pronounced clunk of the other station's carrier, even stronger now than before. Greg reached for the world globe he kept on the windowsill, spun it around to the South Atlantic. Sure enough, there was Ascension Island, a tiny bump just above the "U" in "South." He spanned the distanced their signals were traveling between his thumb and forefinger. It was impressively considerable.

"Greg, copied one-hundred percent," Steve was saying. "Looks like good propagation our way tonight. Of course, the big rhombic antenna I aim at the U.S. helps more than somewhat, I guess. You know, I used to have a Globe Scout myself when I was growing up down in Alabama. My first transmitter. It's probably in my mom's basement somewhere with all my other gear I started up with."

Amazingly, the conversation continued. Steve only missed a word here or there and Greg heard everything ZD8AA said. Everything. How he was an engineer, working for the U.S. space program at a tracking station there. How he got his degree in engineering, even though he hated math as a kid. About how he finally realized the practical aspects of math when he learned about Ohm's Law, studying for his ham radio license, and actually applied it when he built a transmitter and made his first contact on the air with it. The fact it went up in smoke a few days later when the transformer shorted out did not diminish the thrill one iota. Neither did having to replace his mother's bedroom curtains that got smoked in the process.

When they finally said their "73s" ("best regards") and signed off, Greg was far too pumped to do homework. He took his time filling in the blanks in his logbook. Then he forced himself to stare at and concentrate on the neat row of problems on his worksheet for a while before he finally considered trying to solve one of them.

It seemed easy. So did the second one. The third was tougher, but he pictured Steve, sitting before that big transmitter, looking out his window at the ocean with the first rays of daylight sparkling on its surface beyond the big, Erector-set-like satellite tracking dishes. The dishes Steve helped build and maintain.

"Greg, maybe if you study hard and get past that math, you can help us get the first man on the moon," ZD8AA had told him. And as Greg noodled through the more difficult problems at the bottom of the purple-mimeographed sheet, he used those words as impetus to not give up so easily on finding the correct solutions to each.

The next evening, about the same time, Greg warmed up the transmitter on 14.250, dialed the receiver up and down ten kilohertz either side of that spot on the dial, and listened hard. If anything, the band was in worse shape than the night before. Even a couple of schedules he listened to some nights were giving up early, heading for *Gunsmoke* on the television.

No ZD8AA either. So, what the heck?

He touched the crystal for luck, as he always did, muted the receiver, threw the "Transmit" switch on the Scout, and gave Steve a call.

Greg tried to keep the pleading out of his voice when he asked, "Are you out there tonight, Steve?"

Almost immediately, the massive carrier was there, just as strong as before, and ZD8AA was answering his plaintive call. Greg's signal eventually faded to the point that Steve was no longer able to copy him, and several long, slow swoops of QSB (fading) even took Steve's voice to the brink of the noise, but they still managed forty-five minutes of conversation.

Steve described for him what life was like on the remote island, told him as much as he could about what he did at work. Greg kept his comments short, still afraid he would drop off the edge of the ionosphere in the middle of a word and the conversation would be over. But he fished for more inspiration, for more encouragement to follow his dream of becoming an engineer, a scientist, something in technology.

ZD8AA happily obliged.

Greg and Steve talked quite a few times over the next few months. Sometimes propagation conditions only allowed a short chat. Several times, Steve could not pull Greg's signal out of the swamp at all. A couple of times, they dropped to forty meters and CW, and they made quick contacts both times, though not good enough to say much to each other.

Greg was inspired to cobble together a vertical antenna, made from pieces of Mr. Oliver's old TV antenna. The one that got eaten by a tree in a storm. Greg mounted it with a set of radials—with his dad's blessings and assistance—on his roof. It helped considerably.

Greg also built an outboard VFO (variable frequency oscillator, a device that allowed him to change to any operating frequency) for his Scout transmitter so they could move around the band when QRM (interference) threatened. He found a schematic and wired together a pre-amp (receiving amplifier to boost incoming signals) for the receiver, too, but that really did not work. It just allowed strong signals—like Steve's—to swamp the S-38 and make it impossible to hear anybody.

Of course, he had many other interesting conversations with other amateur radio stations on the bands, and his QSL (postcards sent to confirm a contact) collection grew to the point they spilled out of his desk drawer. Still, one of the few cards he Scotch-taped to his bedroom wall showed a picture of a massive tracking dish and the South Atlantic Ocean in the background, and it bore in big block letters the call sign "ZD8AA."

In the spring, at the end of a great QSO in which Steve gave Greg some wonderful tips on comprehending calculus, Steve ended his final transmission rather mysteriously.

"Well, Greg, I know you are about to start that summer job and earn all that money so you can down to Ohio State, so I don't know how much we will be able to talk for the next little while. By the way, we are about to get really busy down here. I can't say anything, but…well…we will be busy and I'm going to have to leave 'Ole Betsy's' filaments off for the most part. But I'll look for you when I can."

Greg did not probe. He knew better by then. Sometimes Steve bluntly told him he could not talk about a particular subject or answer an especially probing question.

The summer job was in construction and some nights Greg was too tired to even turn on the radio. There was a girlfriend or two as well, and friends who did not understand his affection for radio. They often succeeded in dragging him off to other typical teenager pursuits.

It was true, too, that Greg was hardly aware of anything else that was going on in the world, much less on the amateur band. But, when he did have the chance to operate, the thrill was still there any time his little station reached out across the world. Or just across the county.

It was a rainy Wednesday in July. Greg's boss called the night before and said the job would be shut down due to the weather. He told Greg to take the day off.

Wonderful! As badly as he needed to save money for college, Greg was happy to have a rare day off. He planned to get up early and try to catch the ham stations that often came through on fifteen meters from Southeast Asia and Australia and New Zealand about sunrise.

Fatigue won out, though, and he slapped the alarm off when it tried to interrupt his precious rest. Still, he had a hard time sleeping and eventually climbed out of bed anyway. Nothing interesting on the fifteen meter band so he went off in search of breakfast. To his surprise, he quickly found that his mom had not fixed anything for him. That never happened.

Instead, she was in the living room, sitting in Dad's easy chair, leaning forward, her eyes fixed to the TV. Greg had never seen his mom watch anything with such intensity. Anything, that is, but her soap operas.

"Mom, we got any pancake..."

"Sssshhhhh! Come here. I was about to wake you. Watch this."

"But I'm hungry and..."

She kept her eyes on the small, gray screen but waved vigorously for him to come over and watch.

There was a wavy picture of a rocket on a launch platform, white clouds of gas escaping at a couple of points along its flanks. Apollo 11. Greg was dimly aware that there was to be a space mission—an attempt to land a man on the moon—sometime this summer. In the crush of all that had been going on, he had lost track of it all. Still, his heart quickened when he realized what was happening.

"They're going to the moon! Greg, they are going to try to land and walk around on the moon! Who would have thought we would have lived to see this day?"

Her excitement was contagious. The countdown was in the teens already. Then a billow of smoke at the base of the rocket signaled it was about to leave earth, head down range, put Apollo into orbit before she ultimately fired more rockets and pointed toward the lunar surface, over a quarter of a million miles away.

Greg watched, not one bit ashamed of the tears in his eyes, as the mission proceeded right on schedule. His mom hugged him.

"Just think. Someday you will help do things like that," she told him with pride in her voice.

He smiled and kissed her cheek before he headed upstairs. People on the amateur radio bands would be talking about what was happening and he wanted to join in that conversation.

As he sat down and turned on the transmitter and receiver, his eye caught the QSL card on the wall. The one with the tracking dish and the blue South Atlantic in the background and the block letters that said it came from "ZD8AA."

Steve! So that was what was keeping him so busy these days!

His friend, his QSO buddy, was at that very moment helping keep man's first moon mission safely on track, tweaking the knobs and dials just as he did on "Ole Betsy," aiming his dishes at the space capsule the same as he did his rhombic he had pointed toward Cleveland.

Someday, Greg thought. *Someday.* As he smelled the familiar aroma of the tubes in his radios heating up. As he listened to the soft cracking of their cabinets and quiet, comforting hum of their components. As he watched the dial light flicker slightly inside the VFO he had built with his own hands with his uncle's cast-off soldering iron.

Someday.

So the bug bites. You decide to explore the possibility of getting an amateur radio license. I am going to simply make one suggestion here: visit the web site for the American Radio Relay League at **www.arrl.org**.

This is the hobby's national organization and can lead you to myriad resources for getting licensed, assembling a station, and becoming an accomplished ham radio operator. Yes, you do need a license, the examination for which can be administered right there in your area by a group of volunteer examiners. Many clubs sponsor regular examination sessions and the cost is minimal. Others conduct licensing classes, too.

There is a full explanation of the requirements and steps you need to take all right there on the ARRL's site. You will also find news about things going on in the hobby as well as interesting and entertaining videos, news, reviews of equipment, and interesting articles.

I also suggest a couple more web sites getting added to your "Favorites" or "Bookmarks": **www.eham.net** and **www.qrz.com**.

Both sites offer articles, news, a classified section, reviews, license examination practice questions, ads from equipment vendors and manufacturers, and much more that will enhance your enjoyment of the hobby and give you a forum to chat with others who are just as smitten with ham radio as you are. You will feel even more a member of the "tribe" if you frequent these web sites.

You will also see links to many other ham radio-related web sites at these locations. You might even try mine: **www.n4kc.com**. I have links, reviews and some other articles and stories posted there.

Here is another idea. Google "amateur radio club" and stick in the name of your city or area. There are hundreds of active clubs around the country. Most welcome newcomers with open arms. Some do not.

Believe it or not, hams are just like other human beings. There are some great folks in the hobby and there are some slugs. The proportion of good to evil in our hobby is actually much better than in the general populace, I am firmly convinced. Give it a shot, though. Don't let one curmudgeon and his lack of helpfulness sour you on the vast majority of hams who will welcome you eagerly to our ranks.

As far as clubs go, you do not have to be a "joiner," but if you need and want support—especially in the beginning and as you prepare for the FCC examination and get ready to go on the air—a local group is a great place to start.

Later in this book, I will offer some of my suggestions on what you can do to get the most out of the hobby once you take the plunge, do the studying, and pass the exam. I will also talk about some ways to grow in the hobby, and to keep it fresh and fun, even if you get bored with one aspect or the other.

First, though, I know what will be on your mind when you do pass the exam and get that call sign: your station. For many, equipment and an antenna are the biggest impediment to entering amateur radio. There is great trepidation and uncertainty about putting such a monster together.

Many make a very basic mistake by going the easy, uncomplicated route—buy a VHF walkie-talkie with a tiny antenna—and are disappointed with the experience for which they have worked so hard. An HT ("handi-talkie"...that is what we call that little low-powered, handheld VHF radio transceiver) is a nice thing to have, and can be a lot of fun to play with, but with its limited power and compromise antenna, it is not going to give you the best taste of all that ham radio has to offer.

New amateurs assume that the equipment to get on the air will be too expensive. "I cannot put up a tower with a honking big antenna on top of it. My neighbors will tar and feather me!"

"How can I communicate if I don't have top-of-the-line gear for my station and an antenna that reaches halfway to the moon?"

Let me assure you there are ways. Amateur radio is not expensive at all when you compare it to other hobbies. Think about what it costs to fully equip yourself to be a fisherman, with all that tackle, lures, and even a boat. Or invest in a full set of golf clubs, club membership, greens fees, and more.

Truth is, you can spend as much on building your station—thousands!—as you want, but you can also get on the air and have a lot of fun for far, far less. You do not have to have a top-line station when you start out either. It is actually a good idea to wait and see where your interests take you and then build a station around those.

One of the first places you may look to get set up to start out is at one of the amateur radio retailers out there, all of whom have web sites and online ordering. Or at the for-sale pages on the web sites I mentioned above and other places, including Craig's List and eBay.

The following two chapters deal with each of these sources, hopefully in a humorous way. But you will also glean some helpful advice, too.

Good hunting…but caveat emptor! Buyer, beware!

Chapter 2 -- Caveat Emptor: Thoughts While Perusing a Ham Radio Catalog

I have this habit of sitting in front of the rig while waiting for a net to begin or for 15 meters to suddenly and miraculously open to Asia, thumbing through the latest catalog from one of the major amateur radio equipment suppliers or scrolling through their web sites. Doesn't matter which one. They are all basically the same. I suppose it is because I like to dream about the stuff I see pictured there, sort of like when I was in my teens and discovered *Playboy*. And I notice one thing that has not changed since I used to gaze longingly at similar publications from Allied Radio and Grice Electronics way back when Marconi and I were in some of the same on-the-air pile-ups.

You have to take much of what they say with a grain of salt.

Look, Sears Roebuck, in their famous catalog, never said, "This shirt is going to unravel at the cuffs and the buttons will fall off the first time you wash it." L.L. Bean won't print, "These boots are about as comfortable as a pair of cement blocks strapped to your dogs!" Nor will any of the equipment distributors advise, "The SuperGain Ether-Thumper antenna is really just a resistor and a coil, wrapped in epoxy, and will release vast amounts of smoke if you actually send it some radio-frequency energy."

On the other hand, they typically do not tell bald-faced lies either. That would be bad business in a very competitive space and there are a number of alphabet-soup federal agencies that can and do whack them good if they get caught. But I do think it advisable to point out a few things to watch for, for old-timers and new hams who might be joining this wonderful hobby.

The siren call of antenna gain

I recently read a perfect depiction of how antenna gain works: think of a person standing in the middle of an empty parking lot. The person is yelling. Never mind why—this is just a "depiction!" Imagine how the voice sounds if you are a couple of hundred feet away. Now, have someone hand that loudmouth a megaphone and he shouts—at the same level—through it, with it pointed toward you, then away from you. What happens to the level of his voice?

All that depiction stuff is to alert potential antenna buyers (and builders, for that matter) to a typical half-truth they might encounter. I recently saw a page full of antennas manufactured by a well-known company that has been making aerials for decades. There is a nice chart showing all aspects of the various offerings, including one column labeled "Gain." And one of the top models, a multi-band monster priced about as much as a good used automobile, promises "12 dB" of gain. 12 dB! Even newcomers might be impressed with that number. Where is my

Visa card? How quickly can you get that truckload of gain to my backyard?

But think about the guy in the parking lot, shouting his lungs out. How did you know the megaphone made his voice much, much louder when he pointed it in your direction? Because you could directly compare it to how loud his voice was without the megaphone, or when he was turned away from you. What you had was *a basis of comparison*.

Antenna gain is the same way. It is, by definition, a comparison to some other state or condition. Is that attractive gain of 12 dB achieved when the antenna is compared to another mega-dollar model or is it in relation to what you get when you try to emit a radio signal from a can of baked beans?

In many cases you will see a notation or footnote that tells you what the basis of comparison is. In others you won't. Typically, the standard for antennas is an *isotropic source*, a fancy word for a theoretically perfect antenna, with no other factors acting on it. Factors like dirt, air, pollution, or Junior's jungle gym out there in the backyard. Stated as "dBi," this is, in effect, comparing that conglomeration of high-priced aluminum in the catalog to something that could never exist in the real world. But—and this is important—at least it is a basis of comparison, and so long as you use that same basis for each of the high-priced conglomerations of aluminum you are considering purchasing, you are fine (assuming the manufacturer is not telling bald-faced lies or making up stuff). 12 dBi is better than 3 dBi any day!

Sometimes, in the interest of being more open, a figure labeled "dBd" might be used. This refers to a perfect, non-reactive dipole antenna, also arrayed in a vacuum, strung up in free space, a long way from your socks and long-johns hanging on the clothesline. Still, if you compare apples to apples—that is "dBd" to "dBd"—you are okay. Putting up dBd against dBi is problematic. dBi wins every time. That should tell you why some manufacturers only use that figure if they are trying to convince you to come off your wallet and invest in that baby.

And let me hasten to point out that the distributors who publish the catalogs are typically passing along the information provided by the manufacturers, not data from some extensive lab they have on premises just to ferret out exaggerated claims from equipment builders. If I go to the web site for the above-mentioned antenna builder, that same table appears. Incidentally, the gain figures posted are not farther defined on the manufacturer's web site either.

Power supply or chunk of charred flotsam?

So I thumb on back to the pages containing power supplies, since I have considered a 20-amp switching model so I can use an old VHF FM rig that draws better than 12 amps when I'm sharing my vast knowledge with the guys on the local 146.88

megahertz repeater. I see one, and it has not one but fancy two meters on its handsome face, and the adjacent copy proudly proclaims that it loafs along at 20 amps, 12 volts. And the price is less than I could acquire the parts and wire up one for myself.

But what is that fine print way down at the bottom of the listing? I squint and vow to get my eyeglass prescription renewed soon, but I'm finally able to make out what the mice type says: "Current rating is for intermittent modes. Maximum current for high-duty-cycle modes such as FM or AM is 10 amps."

Hmmm. Glad I noticed that little nugget.

Watch your asterisk!

I see several instances in this catalog where specs for a receiver are quoted in big, bulleted prose, but if you follow the asterisk to the bottom of the page, you see those impressive numbers were accomplished with optional and pricey filters or other add-ons. And here's a bright, colorful starburst proclaiming "$300 off!!!" But down there in type so small you need a telescope to read it, it says something about you having to buy some other gizmo you do not necessarily want or need in order to earn the discount. Or you have to pay full price and wait six months for the manufacturer to consider all the paperwork you had to arrange, copy, have notarized and send to them before midnight of the day you bought the thing, all before they will even think about cutting you the rebate check.

I am not accusing anyone of subterfuge. I am thankful every day that manufacturers continue to provide us with such wonderful gear at what are, really, pretty good prices. And that distributors continue to stay open in what has to be a ridiculously low-margin business, and do, for the most part, a remarkable job of getting us our toys as inexpensively and quickly as possible.

But I am just saying. Be careful. Read and compare cautiously. Use the same basis of comparison for each item. Ask. Investigate. Read the reviews on eHam.net and on other sites. Study the lab tests in *QST* while ignoring those alarmists who claim the results are biased because ARRL dares to sell ads in the magazine to companies whose products they test. This information is as unbiased as it can possibly be.

Hey, if you are new to the hobby, welcome. I envy you all the fun you are about to have. And if you are an old-timer about to order up a Whizbang 3000, 1.8-to-440 megahertz, 2-kilowatt rock-crusher of a radio...well, I just plain envy you!

Chapter 3 -- Reading Between the Lines

When contemplating an amateur radio purchase, I find the reviews offered by other users on the various web sites—including those such as eBay—to be quite helpful. After a piece of gear has accumulated several dozen comments, I find there is enough input to make a good judgment about not only the quality of the item but whether its feature set is really what I am looking for. After many years of perusing the reviews, though, I think I have picked up the ability to read between the lines of some of them, and to glean even more information from them.

As a service to my fellow hams, here is a quick guide to what posters are really saying in those reviews.

No need to thank me. I'm happy to help.

What the reviewer says: "This thing is a POS!"

What the reviewer means: "This wonderful bit of electronic engineering is a POS - a `perfectly operating system!' I would buy a dozen but I don't have room to store them."

What the reviewer says: "0/5" rating.

What the reviewer means: "I know the thing has a 4.9/5 average, and I'm the only one—out of 527 reviews—to give it less than a 4. But I pulled mine out of the box, tossed the box and manual in the dumpster, hooked it up, tried to load it up and transmit to a lawn chair, and the output transistors went *pppsssszzzzlll*. What a pile of junk! How can they get away with selling stuff like this?"

What the reviewer says: "I know this antenna is only a 50-ohm resistor in a tub of epoxy, but it is the greatest radiator ever invented. My first contact was with an Australian station on 40 meters in broad daylight from St. Louis. Forget the laws of physics. This technology may well win the Nobel Prize. A hundred years of antenna engineering and never, until now, has someone discovered such a stunning breakthrough like this wonderful aerial. The thing is a miracle!"

What the reviewer means: "My brother-in-law and I make these things in our basement. Every other positive review you see is from somebody we gave a free one in exchange for the `5.' Please buy one. I suddenly have lots and lots of legal bills and the Federal Trade Commission is spamming my in-box."

What the reviewer says: "Too complicated, too many knobs, and the menu structure reminds me of that calculus class I dropped in college. What good is it if I can't figure out how to even turn it on?"

What the reviewer means: "I want DC-to-daylight, roofing filters, noise blanking, all modes, backlighting with a choice of a hundred colors, and instant mode and band-switching, CW speed, mic gain, sideband selection, satellite choices, split and reverse split, three receivers, voice processing, and more...all with two knobs and no menus."

Alternative version of what the reviewer means: "I've been inactive since Nixon was president. I'm still looking for some tubes in this thing. And knobs for the plate and load. A menu on a radio? Next thing you'll tell me is that people are getting radios that plug into their computers. I think I need to go lie down for a while. Did I tell you about my prostate surgery?"

What the reviewer says: "The company's customer service is the worst. I cannot begin to imagine how they even stay in business."

What the reviewer means: "Okay, so I questioned the person's ancestry and sobriety, and used some language more appropriate for a dockworker. And that was just while talking to the receptionist. But their junk blew a fuse and all I did was go key-down for an hour with no antenna hooked up. And fudged just a bit when I told them when I bought it. Fudged by six years. But the least they could have done is send me a new one."

What the reviewer says: "Man, this is one fantastic radio! I had no idea something this great was on the market. I'd buy six more if I had the desk space."

What the reviewer means: "Look, I could have bought a slightly used Toyota for what this box full of parts cost me. It makes power on two bands, drifts like a hobo, smells like sardines when it gets hot—which, by the way, it does quite quickly—and produces transmit audio that sounds like a cement mixer full of gravel. But if you think I'm going to spend that much on something and not pretend to love it, you're out of your mind!"

What the reviewer says: "reel gud flox bt som time seemz to gof wen glocking the qtr. hey, ifn want craigy swartz, this is the wun yu waant."

What the reviewer means: Well, truth is that I haven't quite figured those kinds of posts out yet. I know our education system is superb and that no one could graduate high school without being able to string together a coherent sentence. I figure this must be some other language with which I am not familiar.

What the reviewer says: "WOW! THIS IS ONE SWEET, SWEET PIECE OF HAM RADIO GEAR!!!!!!"

What the reviewer means: "I do like this piece of equipment. I just can't figure out how to get the caps lock on my keyboard turned off since all the RF floating around in the shack turned it on back in `98."

So that is my little attempt at interpreting the web reviews for ham gear. I do hope it has been helpful *and* that you will all continue to give the rest of us the benefit of your comments and experiences with equipment. They do mostly serve a useful purpose, and thanks to the sites that allow for this first-hand commentary.

    Just keep it in perspective, and be sure to read between the lines.

Newcomers can certainly benefit from becoming a bit more familiar with the large amount of spectrum that is available to us amateur radio operators. However, I am often surprised to hear guys who have been around for years who either do not know or give bad advice on what band has what characteristics.

The truth is, regardless the class of license you earn to begin with, there are many, many wavelengths with widely differing traits on which you can operate. Want a quick tour?

Read on!

Chapter 4 -- A Short Guided Tour of the Amateur Radio Shortwave Bands

Not everybody is as wise, experienced, or steeped in ham radio lore as you and I are. Despite dire warnings and a silly AOL article that appeared a few years ago predicting the imminent demise of the hobby, it still seems to be attracting newcomers at a good clip. And although many of you seem to expect it, not every one of the newcomers will know all there is to know about the hobby the first day they apply RF (radio frequency energy) to an antenna.

Many more folks are finding it in their hearts to upgrade to a General Class license, too, allowing them to migrate beyond line-of-sight to much more of the realm of sky wave than they had before. That is who this chapter is primarily for, a primer on what to expect from each band—and a hint or two based on my own experience—that will hopefully have some value for these folks.

If you have been licensed since spark gap, or if you know how to coax P5s and BT7s (prefixes for some really rare countries) out of otherwise dead bands, this chapter is not for you. Skip to the next story or go on about your business.

(But, what the heck? Read through what I have to say anyway. It might just get you off that band where you have been molting since the end of World War II and you will see what else the big, beautiful radio spectrum has to offer!)

That being said, if you are new to the high frequencies (HF)—often called the shortwave bands—then let me highly recommend that you listen to them. Listen! And then listen some more. If you do not get anything else out of this chapter, let that be it. Listening is a great way to learn the nature of the various bands as well as the customs among the natives who typically inhabit them. Yes, customs vary somewhat, megacycle to megacycle, and just as you may want to do as the natives do in a new place you visit so as not to offend, you will want to do the same when you try out a new spot in the spectrum.

Now, let's start our tour at the top (if we are talking wavelength)—the "Top Band" is actually what it is often called—or the "bottom" (if you are talking about frequency). Note that with a new amateur radio allocation coming into effect soon even lower in frequency and higher in wavelength—below the current AM broadcast band—this terminology may well change.

160 meters - 1.8 to 2.0 megahertz

An interesting bit of radio spectrum, this. You can pretty much forget it during daylight hours except for local communications of less than 25 miles or so. It is also quite a challenge in the summer in most places because of its susceptibility to atmospheric static. But when the weather cools, it can be a delightful band for both ragchewing and DX.

It has its technical challenges. A half-wavelength dipole should be about 270 feet long to be efficient here, and that is more space than many can devote. Other antenna types can do well here, and especially vertical radiators. After all, just below the 160 meter ham band is the commercial AM broadcast band. Every one of those guys uses vertical antennas of some sort, with ground radials stretched out below them. But even a quarter-wave vertical needs to be about 135 feet tall unless you employ wizardry like coils and traps. Many swear by the inverted-L, which offers the advantages of both a vertical and horizontal radiator in far less space. I use a full-wavelength loop, which rings the backyard. It does well on paths out to 750 miles or so. I have worked Europe many times with it, but it would need to be higher in the air for real DX.

(Incidentally, if you are new to the hobby, you can Google the various antennas I mention in this chapter, or procure a copy of the *ARRL Antenna Book* for more information than you could ever hope to absorb.)

You will find many long-established roundtable QSOs (conversations) on this band. Some are friendly and welcoming to strangers who are bold enough to break in to their groups. Others will either ignore you or give you an earful that might hurt your precious feelings. I would suggest that you treat a roundtable or QSO on the air on any band much as you would a conversation on the street. See if the regular participants seem welcoming of interruption. If not, go somewhere else. There are plenty of other frequencies available. Do not just burst in and interrupt the flow of the conversation, either. Wait for a lull. But do not be surprised if you are told to go play in traffic.

Note, too, that all legal modes of emission are allowed anywhere on this band. That means you could, if you wanted to, fire up on SSB at 1.805 mHz.

Please don't. There is a long-accepted band plan in effect on each amateur band. Follow it. First, it prevents chaos. Secondly, it is the polite thing to do. And finally, you could probably bellow, "CQ," (calling any station) for hours on that frequency and not have anyone answer you since it is in the middle of the portion of the band for digital modes. Oh, a few guys might tell you where you can shove your microphone. On the bright side, that certainly would confirm that your rig and antenna are working. However, there are far better ways to accomplish that!

What is this "band plan" thing? You did not see any questions about that in the General exam pool of questions? Visit the American Radio Relay League web site and print out a copy.

And stick to it. For the reasons quoted above. But mostly because it is the right thing to do.

80 meters - 3.5 to 4.0 megahertz

"80" is really TWO bands - 80 and 75. On a frequency-vs.-wavelength basis, it is one of our biggest chunks of real estate. That can cause some problems if your antenna system is not broad-banded enough or you do not use some kind of matching device, and you want to work both ends of the band.

Like 160, 80/75 is for shorter distance chats during the daytime—but often out to several hundred miles—and susceptible to lightning static. It, too, gives good sky wave at night during parts of the year. You can literally work the world if you are patient enough and have a good enough setup. You will find most stations using dipoles or variations, but the vertical is a good DX antenna here, too, because of its low angle of radiation. It just will not work as well for closer communicating. There are even some beams in use on 80/75. You may have to employ a '56 Buick straight-eight engine to rotate one of those bad boys in the direction you want to talk, though!

Also like 160 meters, you will hear plenty of good-old-boy roundtables as well as nets, mostly because the band supports regional communications so well. The band has also gotten a reputation for having more than its share of curmudgeons, characters, and just plain goofballs, many of whom use language more appropriate for a billiard parlor. I hear them and you will, too, even though such foolishness is not as rampant as some seem to think. That's why our radios come from the factory equipped with a tuning knob. Use it. If they want to show their ignorance and lack of proper upbringing, allow them to do so without benefit of comment from you.

Nets serve a useful purpose and may or may not appeal to you. Give them a listen and decide for yourself. Avoid causing them interference. It is easier for you and your contact to move up or down a few kilohertz than for a couple hundred of their guys to QSY (change frequency).

If you hold a General class license, you may be inspired to go for the Extra when you see the big chunk of Sing Sideband (voice) spectrum those license holders get on 80/75. Extras can do the voice thing all the way from 3.6 megahertz to the top of the band, 4.0 mHz. And the band plan calls for a "DX window" from 3.79 to 3.8—a slice of the band reserved for long-distance contacts. These are frequencies on which anything other than Amateur Extra class licensees can only listen and salivate when stations in Europe or Oceania are rolling in. There are also some great CW (Morse code) DX opportunities on the low end of the band, but you need the Extra to venture below 3.525 where many of them hang out.

60 meters - 5.330 to 5.405 (or thereabouts)

Now this is an odd little band for a number of reasons.

First of all, it is channelized. On every other amateur radio band, you are allowed to transmit on any frequency you like, not just on certain specified "channels." Up until recently, you were only allowed to use upper sideband but new modes were recently authorized. You are limited to 2.8 kilohertz of bandwidth centered on one of those five channels. And you can only run 50 watts "maximum effective radiated power relative to a half-wave dipole." Huh?

Many commercially available radios will not transmit on 60 meters, nor will you find very many antennas for sale for this band either. As far as I can tell, the vertical and dipole are usually the aerials of choice.

All that being said, this is an intriguing band. It could offer the best of 80/75 and 40 in terms of propagation, and with such limited power, you are on equal footing with everybody else. At least if everybody else is behaving and observing the power limitation. (The power is limited here because we hams share this bit of spectrum with some pretty serious other services and the FCC takes it rather badly if you ignore the rules here). 60 meters would seem ideal for antenna experimenters since whatever you use would not be so massive, and the results not masked by running scads of power.

I listen here sometimes and it seems to support good DX and enough people who enjoy ragchewing that you can usually find somebody to talk with. They all seem to be a polite lot, maybe because of the restrictions presented by channelization and low power. Note also that you only need a General Class license to operate here, too.

You may well find this quirky band right up your alley.

40 meters - 7.0 to 7.3 megahertz

Many proclaim 40 to be their favorite band and there is good reason...except for one big negative. The negative in a moment, and even it has recently gotten much, much better.

No matter your ham radio interest, 40 meters supports it nicely. CW? Plenty of it. Digital modes? It's there, almost all day every day. Ragchewing? You can almost always scare up a conversation, and in my experience, it always seems to be with someone interesting to talk with. Nets? Beau coups! And you will find plenty of them devoted to about anything you can think of, regardless your interests inside or outside amateur radio. DX? Year round during the evening and early-morning hours, and to most all parts of the globe.

Antennas are more reasonably sized here. A dipole is only about 63 feet in length. A quarter-wave vertical can be a bit over thirty feet tall with radials spread out on the ground or in the air around it that are about the same length. Even garden-home citizens can usually find enough room to erect an antenna of some kind for this band. If you experiment with antennas, you can have a blast. Vertical phased arrays. Weird wire antennas with exotic names. Even Yagis become something close to practical for some here.

This is a good QRP(very low power output, usually five watts or less) band, too. Stations running less power than your flashlight can work stations all over the planet here.

This is another band where the Extras can roam free, too, all the way down to 7.125 on SSB. And the lower 25 kilohertz of the band is a CW DXer's dream. As mentioned, late afternoons all the way through an hour or so after sunrise, hams from all over the world communicate to some degree. I have worked well over 150 countries on 40—even in the sunspot-deficient years—with 100 watts and either a vertical, a G5RV antenna, or the big, previously-mentioned loop doing the radiatin'.

One caveat and then that big negative I mentioned. The SSB authorization in many parts of the world do not match up with ours. You may hear a DX SSB station working stateside stations one after the other, but he is transmitting on 7.095 or some other spot below 7.125. Occasionally you will hear a W, N, A, or K calling him on his frequency. Bad form! First, the DX operator will never hear that station because he is listening up...not the 2 kilohertz or 5 kilohertz normally used when DX operates "split." (He transmits on one frequency but listens on another so the mob chasing him does not wipe him out and nobody hears him.) No, he's listening up "100" or up "150," and will usually let everyone know periodically where to call him.

Remember what I said about listening? Anyone from the U.S. transmitting on SSB/voice below 7.125 is operating illegally. Usually it is only because the op forgot to hit the "Split" button on his transceiver and not because he did not know better. At least, I hope so. He's breaking the rules regardless.

So what's not to love about 40 meters? Shortwave broadcasts. They are big and strong and really, really annoying, and you will hear them from 7.200 all the way up to the top. We share 40 meters with shortwave broadcasters in other parts of the world, so they are there legally. It is simply something you will have to deal with if you use this band.

There is good news, though. First, many countries are turning off their shortwave broadcasts altogether. Their audiences have shrunk, and many governments are using the Internet instead. Bad news for what are called SWLs (shortwave listeners) but great news for hams on 40 meters.

Also, several years ago, by international agreement, the broadcasters had to abandon the frequencies on the band up to 7.2 megahertz. "Supposed to" are the key words there. A few stations—mostly heard on the West Coast—continue to ignore the marching orders to move. However, the flight of the bulk of those shortwave guys has certainly made the SSB portion of the band from 7.125 to 7.2 megahertz much more desirable.

And there it is, yet another reason for you to crack the Extra Class study guide!

30 meters - 10.1 to 10.15 megahertz

Now here's an interesting band! If you are a no-code licensee and have not gotten around to learning CW yet, there is nothing here for you. You are only allowed CW, RTTY (radio teletype) and other data modes. If you think you need to make the lights dim throughout the neighborhood when you transmit, 30 is not your cup of electrons, either. You can only legally run 200 watts PEP. Okay, I know some people ignore that rule. I was born at night but it wasn't last night!

But, like the power limitations on 60, this serves to put everyone on more or less equal footing. "Big guns" are the ones who have optimized their antennas, not their linear amplifiers. And their operating skills. Don't forget that difference maker!

Like 40, this is a good DX band, best at night but often offering long-distance contacts in daylight hours, especially in the winter months. And while still a bit high in wavelength for a beam for most of us, it is possible to design some very effective antennas for 30. I have found it to be relatively empty during the daytime, except for RTTY and digital modes like PSK31, but it really comes alive at night.

I also notice quite a few ops using comparatively slow code here. I assume these are guys who simply cannot ignore the treats that 30 meters offers but are not necessarily proficient in the CW. Guys slow down for them, too. This seems to be one of our more polite bands. Only in the most intense DX pile-ups have I heard colorful language used, and even then, unless your 4-year-old speaks CW, he will never know that guy was questioning the marital status of the other guy's parents.

If you hold a General class license or above, the whole 50 kilohertz of this band is yours. It's that "equal footing" thing again.

One other point: if you don't like contests (we call it radio-sport, trying to make as many contacts within a set period as possible) and believe they are the ruin of radio-dom, no problem on 30. As a "WARC band," (so named because they were authorized at a World Administrative Radio Conference a while back), most contests are forbidden here. Same with 60, 17, and 12 meters.

20 meters - 14.0 to 14.350 kilohertz

The king of the DX bands! Long live the king! Treasures abound on this chunk of magnificent propagation. Granted we have to work a bit harder for it when the sunspot cycle (a determinant of propagation on many shortwave bands) is in certain phases, but even with limited power and wire antennas, you will be able to have delightful conversations with stations in Switzerland, New Zealand, or Poughkeepsie. On a recent weekend, while goofing around, I worked two new countries, one in the South Pacific and one in a former Soviet Union country. That was with 400 watts and a homebrew hex-beam. I have worked lots of odd-sounding call signs with 100 watts and a G5RV or a simple, ground-mounted, multi-band vertical.

There are plenty of things to occupy your leisure time, too. Slow-scan TV, RTTY, digital modes, nets, and more.

Granted you are better off with a beam antenna and more power. Power and high-gain antennas rule on this band. Still, many QRP stations have confirmed contacts with ops in hundreds of countries. A vertical is a good choice on this band, and especially if your fancy favors DXing.

Propagation-wise, 20 meters is best for DX around sunrise and sunset, but I work into Africa and the South Pacific at all hours if I am patient enough. It does tend to go to sleep at night during some portions of the eleven-year sunspot cycle, but do not write it off. Just when you think it is dead and worthless, there's a station on some exotic isle somewhere calling CQ.

Like 80/75, this band has its share of malcontents and just plain rude guys with microphones. Ignore the Canadian kook at

14.313, too. There is no sanity test for a ham radio license in that country either. But there are also an abundance of interesting people to talk to. I do not think I have ever had a boring QSO on this band, SSB, PSK31, RTTY, or CW.

Call CQ (after asking if the frequency is in use, of course) and you never know who will come back to you—a rock star, a missionary in Bolivia, the owner of a major amateur radio manufacturer—or even a retiree in Florida! And sometimes nobody. It is easy to get lost in the vastness of this band and the QRM (interference) if you do not have some power and an antenna that helps. People tend to answer CQs from louder stations if they envision a nice, long conversation.

If you are not into contesting, this band might be a challenge. There is likely some kind of radio-sport event going on every weekend, and this is a popular band for such things. The big DX contests and the annual ARRL Sweepstakes render 20 almost unusable for anything else. But the CW and SSB versions of these contests are on different weekends so you can move to the opposite mode (or to digital) and find the band remarkably open with all those other guys trying to contact each other for points and everlasting glory.

Or go to 60, 30, 17, or 12 where no contester can be heard. Better still, jump into the middle of the contest and get your feet wet. These things are great for filling in the blanks in your Worked All States (working and confirming contact with all 50 US states) or DXCC (trying to contact and confirm that contact with as many countries around the world as you can) list. And be forewarned: radio-sport can be addictive.

17 meters - 18.068 to 18.168 megahertz

"The Gentleman's Band." Have you heard that expression used when describing 17 meters? There does seem to be some validity in that description. There is little of the rush-rush of 20 meters here. For a DX band, there are more ragchews across oceans than on other bands, it appears. Even DXpeditions (operators who go set up in locations around the world where there are few or no hams and allow as many stations as possible to work them) seem slightly more sedate when working 100 stations per hour on 17.

17 meters offers very good propagation at times and does not go to sleep nearly as much as its distant cousin, 15 meters. The atmospheric noise seems quieter here than on 20, too. Effective antennas are more modest in size. A mini-beam, hex-beam, or vertical antenna performs well. And power seems to be less an issue.

But as I say this, I tune the band and there is nothing but hiss and a couple of birdies internal to my fine rig. It is 2100 (9 PM) local time and an hour ago, the West Coast stations were booming in with an occasional ZL (New Zealand) coming through.

You can be enjoying a nice chat with a VE7 in British Columbia who is well above S-9 on the meter, and then, in a few seconds and with a "whoosh," he's gone. Then five minutes later, he's back, stronger than ever, talking with a station in Nicaragua. Until he disappears ten minutes after that, just as suddenly.

The band seems less crowded than others, even though it is relatively narrow, partly because of the nature of the propagation but maybe because tri-band beams and many commercially-sold verticals do not work there. My G5RV and my loop work okay on 17 meters, and the hex-beam is great. I could modify my 4-band vertical, too, but why bother? I love turning the hex-beam around and hearing a station go from down-in-the-noise to in-the-room-with-me.

I am not sure why 17 meters does not get the respect or activity it deserves. It is a very interesting band that offers truly exciting propagation at times, and, as mentioned, it performs well even with relatively low power and modest antennas. Plus it is simply quieter than other bands, in my estimation.

15 meters - 21.0 to 21.450 megahertz

If 20 meters is the "king," then 15 is the once and future "king of DX." You tune there most of the time when sunspots are scarce and you hear nothing but vast emptiness. Occasionally it opens to South America or the Caribbean, but mostly it is just "sssssssshhhhhhh." But wait a year or so and it wakes up and gets downright rowdy!

If you like to combine ragchewing with DXing, if you enjoy working Europeans or Japanese stations on PSK31 or RTTY, if you want to close out your DXCC in one weekend, then 15 will be your band when Ol' Sol blesses us with blemishes on his countenance.

Plus there is plenty of room to operate. This band seems to go on forever! There is plenty of elbow room regardless your license class.

By this point in the spectrum, too, the size of an antenna is starting to come down to the point that a full-size Yagi is possible on a postage-stamp-sized city lot. Heck, a dipole is only about eleven feet long on each side of the center insulator. You could stretch that across your patio and be on the air with a decent signal.

There are many relatively inexpensive tri-band beams available and they all cover 15 meters. And despite the sheer size of the band in hertz, it is relatively small in wavelengths, so most any antenna will be efficient from the bottom to the top of this interesting band.

It is true that once the sunspots begin to go into hiding, the band will once again return to "sssssssshhhhhhh." But it is a great ride in the meantime, and just as with other bands, it can surprise you sometimes when you think it is kaput.

Stick something up in the air and join in the fun.

12 meters - 24.89 to 24.99 megahertz

Now this is one odd band! It is stuck in there between 10 and 15 meters, and I once found myself operating it so infrequently that I had to go back to the charts to see where I could legally use which mode. Like its siblings on either side, it appears to be dead, dead, dead much of the time during the sunspot lull. But it will pop like crazy when things start heating up.

Also like 60, 30 and 17, many hams simply are not aware of this band because older gear does not include it at all, many amplifiers do not have it available, or if they do, it is an afterthought and may have input matching problems, and there are no contests—ever—on this band. That means less activity.

I can verify that it sometimes offers surprising propagation, even when the sun sleeps. I have worked most of the major DXpeditions over the last several years here. I have had a nice QSO with a ZL on 12 with no fading at all, and it took place in the middle of the afternoon.

Just don't forget about 12 meters being there. I would love to work you there.

10 meters - 28.0 to 29.7 megahertz

Want to work Jas (Japan) and VKs with 100 watts and a coat hanger? Dream of communicating across the sea with 5 watts and a whip antenna? That is 10 meters at the top of the sunspot cycle.

This band often presents sporadic-E propagation (look it up...it is beyond the scope of this chapter), regardless of sunspots, which allows communication up to several thousand miles. That happens mostly in the spring and summer and for a few weeks in early winter, but can occur at any time. It is also a good band for local communication up to a hundred miles (or more if you have elevation and power) on a regular basis. But then, when the band does open up, it can really mess with local nets and regular roundtables when a station from the Czech Republic or American Samoa tries to check into your local emergency-preparedness net.

This band offers the first real use of propagation beacons (stations transmitting continuously to determine when the band opens up), with a bunch of them just below 28.3. This enables you to learn quickly if the band is open. As with some of the other bands, they may well be propagating like crazy but if nobody transmits, nobody knows it. These beacon stations let you know signals are available.

It helps, by the way, if you know Morse code. That is what they use to identify and tell you where they are located. But even if you don't, and you tune down there and hear them chirping away in spots where there normally are not any signals, then you know the band is open to somewhere and you can cast out a

"CQ"—back up there above 28.3 or below 28.2, of course. This portion is, by general agreement, supposed to be for beacons only.

One more interesting aspect of 10 meters is that there are FM repeaters and simplex available, as well as satellite downlinks. Yep, the same kind of FM repeaters you may be accustomed to at VHF and UHF. It is a real trip to hear guys talking to each other on a repeater thousands of miles away, and you can jump right in and join them. The *ARRL Repeater Directory* lists many of them.

I actually use a couple of repeater output frequencies as beacons, keeping my dial set on one of those frequencies so I can just hit the band-switch button and tell in a second if the band is open to that area of the country.

So there you are, a travelogue of the amateur radio HF (high-frequency) bands. We really should be thankful that we have access to such a broad range of spectrum and that it offers us such a wide variety of conditions and signal propagation.

I think if you give some of them a try, you will discover that each has its own personality and appeal, as well as its negatives. Then, if you like them, you can make sure you have antennas that allow you to fully experience them, and that you add them to your allotted operating time.

If you do not have an interest in any of the ones you do not usually use, fine as well. That is the beauty of the hobby. You can do what you prefer.

But you may not ever find out what you are missing if you do not at least give them all a try.

There was a time when most people entering the hobby of amateur radio either built their stations from scratch or modified military surplus radios in order to get on the air. A company called Heathkit made hay for a while with transmitter, receiver, tuner and amplifier kits that most people could put together successfully, following step-by-step instructions and with a hot soldering iron, even if they had limited technical knowledge. Then several companies began manufacturing radios that worked right out of the box but that still could be easily repaired or modified by technically inclined owners. Or at least they could brag that they could fix or alter their rigs. Those without that inclination did not have to bother. They could get on the air and talk, just as they preferred.

As with most other things technical, things have changed. Today's ham radio equipment is almost as much computer as it is radio. Surface-mount manufacturing has made it difficult indeed for anyone to cobble together anything so elaborate in his basement, or even to dare try to tear it apart and fix it if something went haywire.

This is good in that simple, low-power transceiver kits are still available, and they can also be constructed and operated even by those who have little or no interest in what makes them work. It is also good in that radios with truly amazing capabilities and features can be manufactured and sold for truly attractive prices.

On the other hand, it has made it less and less attractive for experimenters to draw up a schematic, gather parts, and build a station from scratch. Some still do. Most do not. If that is what interests you most about the hobby, have at it. It can be fulfilling and a wonderful learning experience. If not, you can still enjoy the hobby to its fullest without knowing which end of the soldering iron gets hot.

But if you, like the vast majority, do not decide to construct your equipment, what is left in the way of building something that can positively (or negatively—sometimes we learn more from failure than we do from success!) affect your station and the ability to talk to the world? What can you do that gives you the satisfaction of putting something together by hand that allows a chat with someone out there on the other end of the circuit who says, "Hey, your 100 watts are really rolling into Dublin tonight!"

My answer to those questions is, "Antennas." Aerials. Transducers. Radiators. Or whatever you wish to call them. Once you generate radio-frequency energy from your transmitter—but first, as soon as you turn on the power expecting to hear signals pouring out of your receiver's speaker—you rely on that piece of wire or aluminum to do its job...so you can be heard and so you can hear the other station.

The good news is, antenna design, construction, and experimentation can be attractive to hams, regardless their technical expertise or interest. There is also much wonderful help available, on the web and in those old-fashioned things called "books."

The bad news? Few things in our hobby are so surrounded by misinformation and encumbered by so many old wives' tales.

It is also true that few things are as intimidating to newcomers (and even some old-timers, though they would never, ever admit it). When they pass the license exam, they rush out and buy a Whizzinsparker 4000 radio and then realize that the 20-foot-long piece of wire draped across the sofa not only does not rake in any strong signals at all but does plenty of whizzing and sparking indeed when they try to transmit.

Let me say it right up front: few aspects of your station will have as much effect on how much you enjoy your hobby than the type and quality of the antennas you employ. That is true whether your radio is a simple VHF/UHF handie-talkie or a multi-thousand-buck desk-load of a transceiver.

But I will say this too: few things you can do in the hobby will give you as much satisfaction as learning the basics of antennas and their feed lines and putting that knowledge to use in a positive way. I will also hasten to add that you can have a perfectly satisfying experience "on the wind" with a piece-of-junk antenna, too. Just not nearly as satisfying as with a proper antenna, thoughtfully fed.

Because of that importance, I have devoted the next seven chapters of the book to the subject. Let us begin with a story about a group of guys who grew weary of one of their peers who claimed to know it all when it came to antennas, and then came up with a way of teaching him some humility.

Nobody knows it all. Not even Joe Wynn.

Chapter 5 -- The Amazing Disappearing Antenna

They were an easy-going group. Most were longtime friends, some went to high school or college together, others became acquaintances when they first took the test for their amateur radio license and joined the exalted fraternity of hamdom. Some were newcomers, teenagers, young adults, even a few husband/wife teams. Some newcomers were gray-haired, too.

All of them shared one common bond. They were deeply involved in the hobby of ham radio and thoroughly enjoyed being with others who were members of the same tribe.

The brotherhood and sisterhood of the spark!

The group met once a month—on a Tuesday night—in a room at the downtown YMCA for their club meeting. They usually began with a warm-up session while everyone gathered and bragged about the distant contacts (DX) they had made or how great their newly-constructed QRP transceiver (low-power...five watts of output or less) was working. There was some horse-trading, too. That was followed by a short business discussion, and then a program, delivered by a member or a guest, always on topics that might be of interest to the group, old-timers and newcomers alike.

As with all assemblies of human beings, there were those occasional moments when things got testy, when politics sparked a tiff or whoever was delivering the night's program made claims that were disputed by someone in the audience who had a different opinion. But it always ended amiably with a motion to adjourn for a cup of coffee and a doughnut at Krispy Kreme and more chatter, bragging and horse-trading.

Joe Wynn, WB4CDB, was delivering the program one night. His subject was some kind of cobbled-together antenna he had conceived and then modeled on his computer, using the latest software. He had then erected and tested the monstrosity. It consisted of an odd amalgam of copper wire, coax cable, snippets of 300-ohm television twin-lead, a strange circuit at its middle with capacitors and coils soldered together, and a bunch of rope to string it up from tree limb to tree limb. Antennas were always hot topics at the club meetings. There was an abundance of opinions about what worked best and what did not.

Most agreed that a hundred watts or a thousand watts of power output was basically the same, regardless the kind of radio that was generating it. But it was the antenna and the feed line that led to it that took those watts, converted them into magnetic energy, and threw it off into space to reverberate off the ionosphere. The more efficiently it did this beautiful trick of physics, the better. The more efficiently an antenna worked, the more successful an amateur radio operator would be in communicating with others of a similar ilk around the state, the country or the world. There was no argument there.

But the more Joe talked about this odd, ugly duckling of a radiator, the more complicated and obtuse his drawings on the white board became. And the more he pontificated about how great it worked, the more some members of the club frowned, snorted, and exchanged quick glances with each other.

"Now when I first looked at the computer model and saw the specs on this aerial, I was amazed," Joe proudly claimed. If he noticed the doubting looks on some faces out there in the group, he ignored them. "SWR below two-to-one across the 40-, 30-, 20-, 17- and 15-meter bands without having to tune it. A very fat lobe that radiates in practically all directions. And a gain over a dipole of 6 dB. And the thing is only 50 feet long in its entirety. I have been using it for a month now and it is by far the best performing antenna I have ever seen. Anybody have any questions?"

John Carlson—a local broadcast engineer and easily one of the more technically competent among the club members—raised his hand.

"Joe, that's a mighty fine explanation, but that all looks like a mess to me." John was always cordial but he also tended to cut to the chase when he had an opinion on something. "If it really does as well as you say, you must have just gotten lucky. I don't see any way that can work."

"Yeah, I can see the SWR being low," Roger Schwartz chimed in. He was the acknowledged "antenna guru" among the bunch. "That circuit there in the middle and the two-hundred feet of coax is probably going to mask any reflected power, but I bet you could cook a hamburger on that little circuit board after a few minutes of key-down!"

"Seems to me to be way complicated, too," Jack Mainerd jumped in. Jack's antenna farm—which actually grew from the black dirt at his spacious farm south of town—was the stuff of dreams for most of the hams in the bunch. "You could just put up a 65-foot dipole, feed it with ladder line, and hit all those bands just fine without the weight, the parts, and all that precise measuring."

Joe Wynn took the comments in stride. He simply rocked back on his heels, grinned, and folded his arms across his chest.

"All I know is it works. I've got the contacts and the signal reports in the log book to back it up. You'd need a couple of trees in the right place for your 65-foot 40-meter dipole antenna, Jack. And figure a way to snake the ladder line around gutters, cables, wire and stuff to get it inside. Then you have to use an antenna tuner—and you all know how I feel about antenna tuners—to get a match on all of those bands. And you would still have a figure-eight pattern with some really nasty nulls and no gain at all. The same as a dipole because it would be a dipole!"

"Heck, Joe, you can make contacts using a ten-penny nail for an antenna if..." Roger started, but just then, Bob Marx, the club president stood up and interrupted before things went sour.

"Well, Joe, thank you for another interesting program," he said with a smile. "You always bring us a project that will make us think. It's past nine already and some of us have to go to work tomorrow to earn money to support our hobby. Let's give Joe Wynn a round of applause."

Everyone did, including the three men who had challenged Joe's weird antenna experiment. It was true. Those members who were good enough to volunteer to conduct a program were always appreciated. And it was also true that WB4CDB always came up with things that...well...made them think. And shake their heads.

There was the transmitter he built from an old television set that dimmed the lights when he transmitted and emitted a signal that sounded more like an elephant burping. The Morse code "translator" that was supposed to take the characters through a microphone set up next to a speaker and convert them into letters that were displayed on an old Atari game console. Only problem was, it could not tell a dash from a dot, a rather fundamental flaw for such a device. But mixed in were some occasionally usable and practical items, too, and, as Bob Marx noted, it made everyone in attendance think, and thinking inevitably led to learning.

This night, the discussion of what Joe had dubbed his "flotsam and jetsam antenna"—he noted that you could just take the flotsam and jetsam from your junk box and build it—continued over the hot coffee and the sweet pastries at the doughnut shop. John, Roger and Jack all continued to challenge, in a friendly enough way, the theory, complexity, and claimed results of the antenna. And Joe stuck to his guns.

"Best antenna in my arsenal right now, and I've got one of about everything growing out there," he maintained.

As they headed for their cars, the three questioners told Joe and the others goodnight, but they huddled at Jack's car for a few minutes before they all loaded up and headed home.

Nobody noticed the sudden burst of laughter just before they climbed into their vehicles and went their separate ways.

Two nights later, Joe Wynn was goofing around in his "shack," working on some project he had discovered in an old *ARRL Amateur Radio Handbook* from the 1950s. There was a "ding" on the computer indicating someone had "spotted" a DX station (reported, on a special website designed for such a purpose, the presence of a particular station that had come on the air). The station was on some tiny island in the South Pacific and when Joe tuned him, his signal on 40 meter CW (Morse code) was marginally readable, though not nearly as strong as the reporter who had spotted him indicated.

Rubbing his hands together in anticipation, Joe waited impatiently for the old tubes in his amplifier to warm up. He clicked the rotary antenna switch around to make sure he had selected the spot on the dial where the plastic label indicated that his super-duper "flotsam and jetsam antenna" was hooked up. Then he hit the button on his transceiver to send power to the amp so he could quickly tune it up.

There was a brief hiss and just the slightest hint of a spark from somewhere inside the cage that housed the amplifier's innards.

"That's odd," Joe muttered, but he quickly twisted the dials until the arcing ceased. Still, the loading was not nearly as smooth as it typically was.

There were surprisingly few other stations calling the distant one, but it took Joe a good half hour to finally get a response from him, even though the DX station called "CQ" (a call for anyone to answer) several times but did not seem to hear WB4CDB when he responded.

Joe simply chalked it up to poor-but-just-good-enough propagation as he proudly logged the new country and placed a pin in the map on the wall to formally mark the accomplishment.

If it was easy, every ham out there would have confirmations from every country on the planet.

The next night, Joe had a 40-meter schedule on single-sideband with an old friend halfway across the country. They usually had no trouble carrying on a conversation, but this night, his friend could hardly hear him and finally lost him altogether. And the amplifier had been even balkier in tuning up, too.

Now Joe was curious. He disconnected the amp from the AC power and carefully lifted the lid and looked inside. Everything looked all right. No smoke. No sign of the tell-tale black carbon streak that would have indicated arcing damage.

He scratched his chin, considered the possibilities, and finally decided to sleep on it. A new DXpedition was set to be on the air starting the next weekend. They would be operating from a tiny coral reef in the middle of the Dangerous Grounds off Malaysia. It would not take long to see if he had some component going on the fritz. In fact, in Joe's estimation, the easiest way to trouble-shoot a problem was to keep using it until "it released smoke" or made enough noise to easily locate it in the midst of whatever might remain.

It had not occurred to Joe Wynn to check his whiz-bang, Rube Goldberg antenna that stretched across the backyard.

The same antenna that John, Roger and Jack—his buddies from the ham club—had been whittling down a few feet or so each evening ever since the night after the meeting!

After they were certain Joe had turned in for the night, the three men crept into Joe's backyard each evening, untied the rope supports from the trees at each end, and lowered the aerial to where they could reach it. Then they took the wire loose from the end insulators, measured precisely with John's pocket tape measure, folded it back on itself, and carefully twisted it so it would be secure. And they did the same thing on the other end. That effectively shortened it each evening by about four feet on each end without really doing any lasting damage to it. They could always let it back out to its original length after putting Joe in his place and showing him the error of his ways.

The men knew Joe's old watchdog, Sparky, was too deaf to hear them and too lazy to alert his master even if he did. They figured the minimal change each night to the antenna would hardly be enough to be noticed. But then, suddenly, Joe would realize that his wonderful concoction of a radiator was not so great after all.

After the fifth night of antenna modification, John Carlson could not resist it any longer. There had been no word whatsoever from Joe Wynn about any issues with the antenna of which he was so proud. Then John heard him on his morning commute, talking to another station on the club's two-meter repeater. John stifled a yawn—the late-night shortening operation was cutting into his sack time—and broke into the QSO at the first opportunity.

"Mornin', Joe and Mel. How you fellows doing? Joe, what's the latest on your 'flotsam and jetsam' antenna?" he asked.

"Even better than I thought!" Joe responded enthusiastically. "I worked a QRP station in Slovenia last night on 17 and then got three more good ones on PSK31 on 20."

John frowned as he eased to a stop at a traffic light. Had old Joe not yet realized that his miracle antenna was working even worse than before? Or was he just too stubborn to admit his antenna did not work before and was a total failure now. John had an idea. It was time to press the point. Heck, a few more nights and there would be no "flotsam and jetsam antenna" left to trim!

"Hey, that's great. Do you mind if some of us drop by and see her in action this weekend?"

"Not at all," Joe Wynn responded immediately. "I'll be home Saturday, trying to work that DXpedition out in Malaysia."

John grinned broadly, ignoring the lady in the car next to him as she gave him an odd look.

"Perfect. We'll probably stop in mid-afternoon."

John could not wait to tell the others about his chat with Joe and how the guy was so sure his antenna was something special that he was blocking out completely its worsening performance. Just to be sure, the three of them made one more late-night stopover in Joe's backyard on Friday night, but this time, they took a good ten feet off the antenna's length. That only left a few feet of wire either side of the monstrosity Joe had hacked together at its center. Unless that bunch out in the Indian Ocean was using the world's highest-gain receiving antenna and some kind of spectacular noise-reduction gear, there would be no way Joe could ever work them.

Truth was, Roger, Jack and John were beginning to feel a tad bit guilty about the dirty trick they were playing on their friend. Even if they did all agree that he deserved it for being so haughty about his physics-defying antenna. To atone, they stopped and got a bucket of chicken wings and some cold beers on the way over to Joe's place on Saturday afternoon.

Joe's wife showed them into the shack in a corner of the garage where Joe was already busy at the radio, tuning in the distant station and setting the proper split between his listening and transmitting frequency. The three visitors could hear the bedlam of chirps and cheeps from all the hams around the world who were desperately calling the rare operation way out there on the other side of the planet. It was a mess. What little power

Joe's miscreation of an antenna might spit out would be lost amid all that mob of stations trying to get the rare contact on the operation's first weekend.

"How's propagation?" Roger asked Joe.

"Not the best," Wynn replied. "Solar flux is only about 95. I can hear him, though. I think he's coming up some."

The men suppressed grins. Sure he could. With that diminished shrimp of an antenna? Not a chance. Not on 20 meters in the middle of the afternoon, even if they were on CW (Morse code).

Joe punched a button on the front of his radio.

"Back to his frequency," he announced. "I can see a few holes in the pile-up on the spectrum scope so I'll call him on one of those frequencies."

With the chicken wings spread out on the corner of the operating desk and with each of the hams enjoying the cold beer, they each listened to the frequency where the faraway station was supposed to be transmitting.

There was nothing. Nothing but the hiss of atmospheric noise.

Jack Mainerd dropped a chicken bone in the trash can, turned his head sideways, and said, "Joe, I don't hear him. You sure you are on his frequency. There are lots of stateside guys calling him so I figure we would at least be able to..."

But just then, there was the sound of rapid Morse as the rare station's operator sent, "N4KC, 599," and then, three seconds later, "R, TU, UP." (The DX station has just acknowledged hearing the call from station N4KC and gave him a signal report, then confirmed he heard a report from the calling station, said, "Thank you," and indicated that he was listening for calls up a few kilohertz in frequency.)

All three doubters looked at each other. The station was actually quite strong. Stronger than he had been at any of their houses an hour before. Propagation must have improved since then. He had to be booming in for Joe to hear him that strong on his junk antenna. Roger Schwartz glanced at the labels on Joe's antenna switch. Sure enough, it was on the position that said "Flotsam/jetsam."

Wynn was already busy pounding out his call sign on his ancient J-38 straight key. Joe did not believe in computerized CW keying or using his radio's CW memory to save info that could be transmitted merely by hitting a button or keyboard key. True CW operators did it the old-fashioned way, with an arm-numbing straight key.

The DX operator answered another station, a W6. Then three Japanese stations in a row. Jack, Roger and John settled back in their chairs, sure that Joe could call all day and all night but would never be heard. Not with all his RF power likely eaten up in heat in the mess of an aerial he was using. They had already decided to let him try long enough to make their point about the ineffectiveness of his homebrew antenna and then gently let him off the hook with an explanation of what they had been doing.

"Anybody ready for another beer and some chicken...?" John started.

But just then, out of Joe's radio speaker, the DX station clearly sent, "WB4CBD, 599." Joe raised his hand to quiet John and calmly—as if it was no surprise at all that the operator had managed to pull his signal out of the wall of stations that were calling him—sent back a maddeningly slow, "599, TU."

All three visitors sat there, eyes wide, jaws dropped, as Joe turned and smiled at them.

"And that was without the amplifier," he said, beaming. "I had a grid resistor go bad and I haven't had a chance to fix it yet. I just worked that guy with 100 watts. And on the fifth call, too." Joe did not seem to notice the amazed looks on his visitors' stunned faces. "That antenna has just kept getting better and better. Don't know why it's changed since I first put it up, but it's hotter than blue blazes now."

John Carlson stood and walked to the garage door and on out into the backyard. Sure enough, most of what he saw stretched across the yard was rope, not copper wire. Joe's antenna was only a small pair of wires and the junkbox-in-a-bundle at its center. He looked at the antenna then back through the window at the radio. At Joe and at the other two hams.

"Well, I'll be," was all he could manage.

He stepped back into the shack, settled into his chair, and studied the fine print on the beer can. Maybe they had somehow made the antenna better by making it smaller. Odds were against such a phenomenon. No way that should have happened. But maybe. Still, they were all baffled. It just did not make sense.

"Hey, there's Pitcairn Island on 14 dot 007. Let's give him a try," Joe said and made his call. The VP6 came right back, and he gave Joe the highest possible signal report, 599, as well.

"Now he's just showing out," Jack whispered.

They watched as Joe made a few more impressive contacts before they all suddenly stood and told him they had to go.

""We all have to try to work the DXpedition, too," John explained. "And I have to tell you, Joe, I think I'm going to try to put that antenna contraption of yours together, too. Maybe a little shorter than how you drew yours up. But I have to admit, that baby works!"

Roger and Jack nodded. Reluctantly, sincerely.

As they left, Joe Wynn thanked them for the wings and beverages and wished them luck on working the DXpedition. Then he watched them go, a sly grin on his face. Watched them as they paused in the driveway and studied his "flotsam and jetsam" antenna for a long moment, pointing, shaking their heads, even arguing with each other. Watched as they shrugged their shoulders before climbing into Roger's car and pulling away.

Finally, sure the doubters were not going to come back, Joe Wynn leaned over to where his antenna switch was bolted to the back wall. He pulled off two of the labels, one that read "Flotsam/jetsam" and the other one that said "Beam." He moved the labels back to their rightful spots on the switch, where they belonged.

To the place where his abysmal, recently shrinking, junk box antenna was hooked and the other to the position on the switch where his five-element Yagi beam—the one mounted at the 100-foot level on his tower, and the antenna he had actually just used to make those impressive contacts—was attached.

The smell of the chicken wings had lured Sparky into the shack. Joe leaned down and scratched the dog between the ears. He handed the mutt one of the wings.

"You deserve this, old boy," he told Sparky. "I do appreciate you bringing me my present last night, buddy."

Joe pulled from his pocket a metal tape measure. Etched in its side was the amateur radio call sign that belonged to John Carlson.

"You know what I always say, Sparky," Joe told his watchdog. "The best antenna is always the one you got!"

Chapter 6 -- The Top Five "Get on the Air Quickly" Antennas

Some of us give up too easily. Or we are too timid to give something new a try. I have seen several examples of this lately. One was a relatively new amateur radio licensee who got all excited after he passed the test to upgrade to a license class that would allow him to talk to the world on the high-frequency bands. He rushed out and acquired and hooked up a perfectly adequate HF station. However, he has so far not gotten around to erecting any kind of decent antenna to use with it. I do not know if is because he is intimidated due to lack of knowledge about antennas or if he simply is not sure what type of antenna to put up. Maybe he hesitated, thinking he should wait until he had arrived at the perfect choice, or something that would elicit "ooohs" and "aaahs" from the stations he would someday talk with. It could even be that he is worried about what the neighbors—or, let's face it, his wife—will think should they look out their kitchen window and see a spider web of wire across the fellow's backyard.

You old-timers should be able to think back a hundred years ago when you first got your ticket. All this stuff was a lot to take in at the beginning. Lots of decisions to make. And not a lot of experience and knowledge to go on.

Here is another example. I know of a long-time ham who came back from a period of inactivity, dragged the old gear out of the closet, and then, for whatever reason, never quite got around to the most important part of the station—the antenna! He threw some wire out the window but could hardly hear anything. His very nice and fully capable radio just hissed at him when he tried to tune up that decidedly inadequate radiator.

I confess I am a procrastinator. I tend to spend a long time getting ready to start to begin to commence to think about launching a project until I inevitably forget what it was I wanted to do. And, by the way, what did I buy those parts and rope and wire and fiberglass and aluminum for in the first place?

But this is different. People who may be otherwise enthusiastic about starting or resuming the hobby are allowing fear or hesitancy to keep them on the sidelines. I am afraid that some of us who attempt to "Elmer" them sometimes contribute to the problem ("Elmer" is both a noun and a verb, either a person who willingly advises and encourages newcomers to ham radio or, as a verb, the act of doing so, a term we often use. However, I prefer "mentor" since "Elmer" sounds a bit old-fashioned to some and might not necessarily convey the best image to some folks these days who picture hams as old guys in flannel shirts, locked in their basements with spitting and sparking radios all around them.). We push antenna ideas that are beyond their means, knowledge or geography and that leads to frustration and discouragement.

Or even sometimes we advocate antennas that are beyond their interest level or desire for learning. Not everyone wants to be an RF engineer or know every aspect of antenna theory. They just want to work some DX or conjure up a rag-chew. There is nothing wrong with that!

In that spirit, I would like to list below what I would recommend as the five best get-on-the-air-quickly-and-easily antenna ideas. Maybe some of you have other suggestions, but understand that I am applying the following logic in picking these particular ones to tout in this book:

--They should be easy to build for most anyone who is willing to try, regardless their skill or knowledge.

--They should not require any special tools or test equipment to construct and tune.

--They may be crafted from easily available materials and cost very little, so there is not much downside if you mess them up.

--They are not necessarily the be-all end-all of RF radiators but they do work well enough to give a good experience to the user.

--They are not necessarily the best for all situations, including for use in antenna-restricted neighborhoods or in condos and apartments. Several of these could, however, be adapted to many of those sorts of situations with a little ingenuity.

--And if someone attempts to construct one of these bad boys, he or she will possibly learn a little antenna theory by osmosis and, just maybe, will become curious enough about the subject to learn more and try more challenging projects.

Now, in no particular order of preference, here are my top five get-on-the-air-quickly-and-easily antennas.

#1 - The half-wave wire dipole

This one is about as basic as it gets and it can work quite well on any band, even six and two meters in a pinch. It consists of two pieces of conductive wire stretched end-to-end, and joined together in the middle with a short bit of insulating material between them. We call that the feed point because that is where your feed line will hook into the antenna itself—where it will "feed" the antenna radio-frequency energy. Insulators and lengths of rope are attached to each of the opposite ends to support the antenna.

You may hear some people refer to this as a "flat top" antenna or a "doublet."

It can be hung between two supports—often trees, sometimes masts, the eave of your house, or anything that will not fall over—and runs parallel to the ground. It can also be supported in the middle so it does not droop down. Or supported in the middle with the ends sloping downward to shorter supports in an inverted or upside-down "vee" configuration. For some reason, this is often called an "inverted vee" antenna. If you remember geometry, it might be obvious to you that the inverted vee takes less space, end to end, than the flat top does. That makes it a good choice if you do not have enough distance between your end supports.

Hams have come up with all sorts of ways to get those two end ropes up high in trees. You will see examples of using slingshots, bow-and-arrow, air guns and other devices to try to get the supports across as high a limb as possible. One caveat here: be careful. An arrow or a lead weight hurled from a slingshot can be lethal and destructive.

This antenna can be fed with coax, such as the popular and relatively inexpensive RG-8X, which is easy to run from the middle of the dipole to your shack. Though it may have more loss than some other types of feed lines, the amount of your precious radio energy that is lost in a hundred feet or so of RG-8X is negligible. The convenience, low weight, cost and other factors make RG-8X a good choice for a dipole.

The center conductor of the coax is soldered or clamped to one leg of the dipole and the shield of the coax is attached to the other. There are several commercially available center insulators that allow you to simply screw your coax onto the insulator if the feed line already has a connector attached to it. They also have a hole in them that allows you to support the antenna by rope in the middle as well as at each end. However you do the middle, be sure you weatherproof it as best you can. You do not want water seeping into the coax as it can lead to unacceptable losses and eventually ruin the cable entirely. Sealant tape and other waterproofing materials are available at your neighborhood big-box hardware store.

    Copper wire is usually used for the wires—we will call them "elements"—for a number of reasons. Most amateur radio equipment dealers sell wire that is specifically intended for dipoles and other wire antennas, but you may have other sources, too. With the price of copper where it is as of this writing, you may have little luck scrounging any discarded wire off electricians or others as we once did. Do use good wire if you can. Wire that will not kink, break or easily corrode, and to which you can easily solder or clamp. But use whatever you have or can get.

    The gauge (diameter) of the wire is not that important so long as it is big enough to adequately support the antenna without breaking—including the center insulator and that coax feed line hanging down from the middle—but is not so big and heavy that it droops or snaps off your supports. The support ropes on each end (and in the middle if you use a center rope to hold it up, too) should be weather and UV resistant (resists the sun's rays) unless you really enjoy reattaching them often and tossing them back over the limb every time the wind blows.

As with most antennas, the higher in the air you can get a dipole, the better, if you want to work distant stations. You will make contacts, though, if it is just above head high, and in some cases it actually works better over closer range than if it was way up there in the clouds. Antennas near the earth tend to send their signals straight up. Then they bounce off the ionosphere right back down to your general area, which can have an advantage if you only want to work out reliably a few hundred miles, such as in a regional disaster net or if you chew the fat most of the time with the same bunch of guys around the state where you live.

On the other hand, you do want to get the antenna high enough so people and animals cannot run into it, hurting themselves and wrecking your nice antenna. That includes the ends if you hang up an inverted vee. There is another worry when you are transmitting. Even with modest transmitter power, there can be enough voltage in certain points along the antenna's length to give somebody a jolt. Bad form, and not very neighborly to zap your next-door neighbor's kid!

The overall length of your two pieces of wire is determined by dividing 468 by the desired operating frequency in megahertz. Results are in feet, so convert if you are metrically oriented.

This means a dipole cut for 3.8 megahertz (near the middle of the 80/75-meter band) will be about 123 feet long, or each element will be about 61 feet 6 inches. You would need supports (trees?) at least about 130 feet apart with no obstacles between, although you can bend the legs around stuff if you really need to.

PROS: Cheap, easy to put up, works well on the band for which it is cut, and if it falls down, you can just put it back up. If it breaks, splice it and put it back up. You can bend the legs to fit on your lot, too. It is also relatively stealthy since it is difficult to see when it is stretched among trees. You might be able to fit one for 40 meters or higher in an attic or beneath an eave on the house, even if you have to bend one or both of the elements. The antenna you have is better than one you do not!

CONS: Needs to be high in the air for DX, is directional to some extent but with little or no gain on its fundamental frequency, and will only be close to resonant on odd multiple harmonics. That means your 3.8 megahertz antenna will probably only be useable on that band unless you use a wide-range antenna tuner between your radio and the feed line. A dipole cut for 7.1 megahertz would work okay on the high end of 15 meters but would be problematic on other bands. Coax feedline can have lots of loss if your antenna presents a lot of reflected power (what many call "SWR"), so even if your tuner makes it work so your transmitter successfully matches the antenna, you may have noticeable loss of power and less than stellar results.

There is a way around that little concern.

#2 - The doublet, but fed with parallel feedline

An effective radiator since the beginning of the hobby, this antenna is really just a dipole, as described above, but instead of using coax to carry the RF to the antenna feed point, it is fed with open-wire feedline, ladder line, or window line. This is a special kind of feed line in which the two conductors are kept the same distance apart from antenna to shack, usually with plastic spacers or some other kind of non-conductive material.

I will not get too technical here, but the characteristics of how coax is made—a center conductor, surrounded by insulating material, then a layer of braid, all covered with non-conducting sheathing—does not handle reflected power very well. If your antenna is not resonant—and it will only be resonant in a very narrow stretch of the spectrum on which you can legally operate—you will have reflected power. Also, since the dipole antenna is a "balanced" radiator and parallel feedline is, in fact, a pair of parallel conductors (balanced), they really like each other.

There are a few issues with parallel, open-wire feed line, though. Since there is no shield around it, you must be careful to not allow it to run near anything metal, or to run it along the ground. You cannot coil up any excess length of it either. I will discuss the positives and negatives of this type feed line in more detail later in this book.

PROS: In addition to the pros of the dipole already mentioned, this antenna also works well on most bands above the one for which you cut it, not just those that are even multiples of the frequency for which it was trimmed to be resonant. That means you should make it as long as you can to increase the amount of the spectrum on which you can use it. Since the parallel feedline typically has very little loss even when the reflected power/SWR is high, the antenna becomes a good multi-band antenna when fed with this type line and used with a wide-range antenna tuner. A so-called "balanced" tuner is even better.

CONS: Open wire feedline must be kept at least a few inches away from metal or other conductors, including the ground. That makes it problematic running the stuff into some shacks alongside coax, beside runs of coax, adjacent to air conditioning units, or near gutters. Since most modern radios have 50-ohm unbalanced outputs, you will need a balun to make the transition from balanced antenna and feedline to unbalanced radio. (Read up on baluns. They can make life easier or more difficult, depending on whether or not you understand them and how they work.) The length of your feedline is also a factor in how the antenna tunes. You may need to experiment to get the correct length for best results on the most bands. (Do not necessarily look at this as a "con," though. This can be fun and a good way to learn more about how this mysterious RF stuff behaves.)

#3 - The quarter-wavelength vertical

A vertical radiator has several advantages over horizontal antennas, including casting out and picking up radio-frequency waves in an omnidirectional manner, having a low-angle of radiation (trust me, this is quite often a good thing for DX), and taking up minimal space. It also allows hams in zoning- or covenant-restricted neighborhoods to put up an effective antenna...if those restrictions allow, for example, the erection of a "flagpole." (A friend of mine has a very fine performing vertical "flagpole" antenna in a neighborhood with very tough restrictions that forbid any type of outdoor antenna. No one complains about his flagpole!)

Plus, a vertical antenna can be as simple as hanging a piece of zip cord from a tree limb. Of course, the wire needs to be insulated from the tree and run some distance away from any other metallic object such as an aluminum mast, tower, or other conductive supporting structure.

The formula for the vertical antenna's length is 234 divided by the frequency you plan to use in megahertz. That's right. The number you use is half as much as the half-wave dipole above. That is because the vertical antenna is a quarter-wavelength long. For 40 meters, the vertical radiating element (wire, aluminum, a flagpole...anything you can hook one side of coax to) is about 33 feet.

Got a tree limb 35 feet off the ground? Tie a knot in a 33-foot-long piece of copper wire, run a rope through the knot, and throw the rope over the limb, tying it off to the trunk. Pull the wire up until the lower end of the wire is three to six inches from the ground.

So far, however, what you actually have is only half of your antenna. To work, you will now need to install the other half.

Lay out pre-cut pieces of wire that are approximately 33 feet long, stretching each one outward from where the bottom of the vertical wire hangs, arraying them in a radial pattern. Use 20 or 30 wires, which we will call "radials." Are 20 or 30 enough? Can you get by with 4 or 8? Yes and yes. But getting at least 20 is a good thing and then you begin to get diminishing returns. Getting more short radials is also better than fewer long ones. Tie the radials together where they all come together in the middle, just beneath the vertical element dangling from the tree limb. Now solder the shield side of some RG-8X to where the radials are twisted together. Solder the center conductor of the coax to the bottom of the hanging wire. Weatherproof it as best you can so no water gets into the coax and is wicked up by the shield, as it tends to do.

Trench out a shallow ditch and bury the coax (make sure that the type coax you use is approved for burial beneath the ground) to a point where you can run it into your shack. Note: you may need to put a balun or some toroids (another one of those terms you should Google and learn more about) on the feedline to keep RF from traveling along the shield, thinking it is just another radial.

That's right. Sometimes the feedline looks like another radial and can pick up stray RF and conduct it into the shack. Once there, it can cause cussing and angst.

There are several commercially made verticals that offer more strength than your wire hanging from a tree, and, through the use of traps or other technology, make them multi-banded. I use a commercially manufactured vertical antenna with traps on 40, 20, 15 and 10 meters and it is a good antenna in many respects. I bought it used for $50. But note that you still need a radial field under any quarter-wavelength-long vertical antenna that is ground-mounted, no matter what the sales pitch says. I have about eighty radials under mine, all covered over by grass and thatch, but that is probably more than I really need.

Yes, a vertical can be mounted above ground, usually on a mast, and this has its benefits as well. You still need at least two radials for each band you will operate on, and for best results, they should cut to be a quarter wavelength long for each band, using that 234-divided-by-the-frequency formula from above. You may even need to do some tuning on those radials, cutting or lengthening them to get the lowest SWR. (However, please do not worry about 1.5- or 1.7-to-1 and spend hours of perfectly good operating time trying to get it flat! No radio minds SWR of 2:1 or better. Again, more on the shadowy world of SWR later.)

If you have a multi-band vertical mounted above the ground, there should be a set of radials for each band that you use (a 40-meter radial will suffice for 15). Getting the antenna up and tying off those radials can be a chore, though.

PROS: A simple and effective antenna, it is omnidirectional. Since it is vertical, it takes very little space to erect, even with a radial field laid out beneath it. Many hams raise them up when they want to operate and lower them when not on the air to keep neighbors and the homeowners' association calm. The angle of radiation is most conducive to working longer distances. Commercially made verticals are available and are quite inexpensive.

CONS: It is omnidirectional, so you reel in signals from and cast out RF into all directions, not just the one in which the station you want to work happens to be. It is also more susceptible to manmade noise than a horizontal antenna, and unless you live on an isolated farm, that is more and more of a consideration these days. It really should be at least a quarter wavelength long for the band on which you want to operate, which means 130 feet tall for 160 meters or 65 feet tall for 80/75. There are electrical ways to make a shorter antenna "appear" longer, but that makes the simple vertical not quite so simple. It requires a radial field...the more wire the better...so you may not have enough real estate to stretch out radials in all directions that are equal to the height of the vertical radiator. (You can cheat on this some, making them shorter or bending radials or not even having them at all where the swimming pool or your neighbor's wooden privacy fence is.) If the vertical is elevated, you need two radials for each band on which you will use it, and that can mean having to find supports for a number of elevated wires. It can take quite a bit of wire if it is ground-mounted! The feedline also needs to be buried, and it can pick up stray RF and ferry it right into your house.

#4 - The horizontal loop

One of my personal favorites, the horizontal loop, can be a good performer, stealthy, and will fit on many smaller lots that a full-size, half-wavelength dipole will not. A loop is just what it sounds like: a big loop of wire, hung horizontally, supported by anything you can find to hold it up it as it makes its way around the backyard or the entire lot where your house sets. Many hams tack the wire beneath the eaves of their house all the way around.

Others erect poles or masts at four corners and make a square loop. You do what you have to do.

When you bring the two ends of that big, long run of wire together at the feed point, you use a short insulator to tie them together, leaving a gap. One conductor of the feedline is attached to one end, the other side to the other end. You can feed with coax or open wire feedline, but open wire is a much better choice if you want to use the antenna on bands where it is not resonant. Good news: the loop will be resonant on all harmonic frequencies, not just the odd ones. That means a loop cut and trimmed for 7.1 megahertz will be close to resonant on 14.2, 21.3, and 28.4 megahertz, all nicely placed in the midst of the 20-, 15- and 10- meter amateur radio bands.

For a resonant loop, the wire length should be calculated using the formula 1005 divided by the frequency in megahertz. A loop cut for 3.8 megahertz is about 264 feet long. A perfect loop is arrayed in a circle, but a square, diamond or rectangle shape is fine, so long as the rectangle is not too "skinny." If you plan to use the loop on multiple bands, simply make sure it is cut at least as long as needed for the lowest frequency on which you intend to operate.

Like the dipoles, a loop performs for DX better if it is higher in the air.

PROS: One of the quieter choices for an antenna, it ignores much of the ever-present manmade electrical noise. It can often fit on real estate that a dipole will not, such as small, narrow or odd-shaped lots. This is especially true when you consider that its shape does not necessarily have to be round. (Example: that 40-meter loop mentioned above, if arrayed as a square with supports at its four corners, would only be about 66 feet on each of its sides. That should easily fit on most suburban lots.) The loop can be supported by whatever trees or other structures you happen to have handy. You do not have to rely on trees or other supports being strategically placed on your lot. And if you use insulated wire, you can run it through trees and bushes with little effect, even if the wire is touching foliage all around. It also has useable gain, especially above the fundamental frequency, with lobes that increase in number as you go higher in frequency. Use open wire or ladder line to feed the loop, employ a wide-range antenna tuner, and it becomes a wonderful multi-band antenna.

CONS: That much wire can be heavy, causing it to droop on long runs. It also requires maintenance since lots of things can happen to a stretch of wire that long (a 160 meter full-wavelength loop is almost 560 feet long!). It can certainly snag lightning, too, and even blowing dust, rain or snow can create a lethal voltage static charge at the end of your feedline. Make sure it is grounded—outside—in such weather, or investigate the various means of bleeding off static charge buildup from such an aerial. With those gain lobes mentioned above, you also get nulls. If the station you want to work is in the middle of a nice lobe, super! If he is in one of those deep nulls, "Sorry, old man, you're down in the mud and I cannot copy you at all!"

#5 - The G5RV

The most discussed, maligned and misunderstood of all the simple antennas! Introduced by a British ham with the call sign G5RV, it has gotten a bad rap because so many manufacturers claim it to be an all-band antenna, "using only your rig's internal tuner!"

Well, no.

By generally accepted definition today (and I urge you to learn more in the *ARRL Antenna Book*, where I got this description, or by using Google), the G5RV is a 102-foot-long dipole, fed with a matching section of 450-ohm window line, and then it uses coax from the end of the ladder line the rest of the way to the shack.

In my experience, the G5RV will work fine on 40 and 20 meters, is not bad on 17 or 10, and might work okay on a narrow portion of 80/75, using only the typical internal automatic antenna tuner in most of today's radios. I can tune it with a good external tuner on other bands but it is mediocre at best and the internal tuner in my rig merely fusses and refuses to even try on those bands. (In all fairness, my G5RV is a derivative version that is 6 feet shorter than the classic version.)

Google "G5RV" for several construction articles. There are also G5RVs available that are commercially made but I cannot vouch for any of them. I would be leery, though, of any that claim "all bands with your rig's internal tuner!" I will also have more later on how to interpret the claims of various manufacturers and equipment dealers.

To get on the air the same day I bought my transceiver several years ago, I purchased a kit from a prominent ham radio antenna-supplier for less than the wire, ladder line and insulators would have cost me had I bought them separately. It took me less than an hour to put it together and only a few more minutes to get it up in the air between a couple of conveniently-placed trees in my backyard. It has been up ever since and is sometimes my best antenna on 40 meters and does quite well on the other bands mentioned above.

PROS: Makes a good antenna on several ham bands, yet it is shorter than a dipole for 80/75 for those with limited space. On 20, it produces four gain lobes in a cloverleaf pattern, which gives you a very good signal in those four directions. It is cheap and, if you follow measuring instructions precisely, it is easy to build and hang. It can be used in an inverted vee configuration, too, if you lack the room or end supports in the proper locations.

CONS: It is not an all-band antenna, any more than any length of random wire and feedline is an all-band antenna. You could create some problematic mismatches, even for a good tuner, if you do not follow recommended measurements closely. The window line should hang down vertically as far as possible so it is best to be able to get the feed point up in the air at least 45 feet or so. And since a portion of the feedline is coax, it will be lossy if you have a high SWR, as mentioned before. Keep the coax as short as possible.

So there they are. The best (in my opinion) and easiest antennas to enable you to get on the air in a hurry. As mentioned, the main reason for this exercise is to give the new ham or someone who is returning to the hobby a bit of inspiration and some choices to consider for an antenna. And to urge them not to be too ambitious—ambitious to the point they never get around to putting anything up!

I think many of you will find a great deal of satisfaction in building your own aerial and then seeing how it works. It is a thrill to have a station on the other side of the continent tell you that you have a really good signal and then be able to tell him, "Thanks! It's homebrew. I built it myself."

There is certainly more satisfaction in that for many of us than there is in buying something already built and simply draping it over something in the backyard. And, as mentioned, antennas is one area where anyone with any technical interest at all can still build, experiment and innovate.

I do encourage you to play with your design. Try things. If it helps, keep it. If it makes your antenna a dummy load, toss it and start over.

But most of all, have fun.

I have heard it said that technological knowledge doubles every five years. That means we are faced each day with technology that is snowballing down a hill and threatens to wreck the village below if we do not keep ahead of it. I often say that anyone who cannot handle rapid change must be living a miserable existence. Change is inevitable.

But with that being said, we can often go back and look at relatively ancient technology and garner some insight into what might still work quite well for our own particular situation. That certainly applies to the world of antennas and their development, implementation, and use in amateur radio.

With cellular technology, satellites, space communication and more, the methodology that Marconi and other wireless pioneers developed has most certainly evolved, and those guys might not recognize how their inventions are being used, even by we amateurs. And yet, on some levels, it is still the same theory they applied, only modified to fit the needs of today and to mesh with all that rapidly changing technology.

That is why I like to remind everyone—with their software defined radios, smart phones, and satellite communications—that there are still plenty of lessons we can learn from the old-timers *when it comes to maximizing the amount of radio energy we can shove out of our antenna systems.*

Chapter 7 -- Lessons from the Old Timers

Down here where I live, we know that three things inevitably lead to fistfights:

--Where your loyalty lies when it comes to college football.

--Which rib joint has the best barbecue.

--And which route offers the quickest trip to the beach.

On the ham bands and in Internet forums, there are at least three equally incendiary topics, guaranteed to get everyone riled up and trashing each other and their heritage:

--Contesters "crowding the bands" and wiping out weekly schedules and long-standing networks.

--The FCC dropping the Morse code requirement for new licensees.

--And whether an antenna that is carefully cut to resonance radiates better than one that is not.

Do not think these are hot topics? Then you have not been listening or reading! I will leave the first two alone for now so I can foolishly—and at risk of "flaming," personal attacks, and questions about my heritage—take on the third topic. I do such a silly thing primarily for three reasons:

--We are enjoying an influx of newly licensed and newly privileged HF operators who might be able to benefit from a rational discussion on the subject.

--We now have TEN amateur radio HF bands, and extended Advanced/Extra SSB privileges that challenge the bandwidth of most antenna system installations, especially on 80/75 meters.

--And as a student of history, I maintain that we can learn valuable lessons from those who came before us. The old timers who pioneered radio were correct on lots of things, including methods for getting the most from limited antenna systems.

Here is the contention of many otherwise knowledgeable hams: you are always better off using an antenna that is cut to resonance for a particular operating frequency. That claim, many say, should be engraved in stone. It is one of the great truisms in the mysterious realm of radio communications.

"Resonance." It sounds like such a nice word. "We are in resonance on that issue, my friend." "That topic resonates with the people!" Dictionary.com defines the word thusly: "To reinforce oscillations because the natural frequency of the device is the same as the frequency of the source." Who could possibly argue with such a wonderful purpose? Don't all we hams want to reinforce oscillations? I know I do!

To cut to the chase, when talking about antenna systems, we call them "resonant" when the capacitive reactance present in the system is equal to the inductive reactance, and the two cancel each other out, leaving the impedance at the load point at its design value—typically 50 ohms. In that magic alignment delivered to us by the gods of RF, the antenna is able to radiate into space most of the radio frequency energy that is sent to it from the transmitter via a feed line.

It is also true that everything seems predestined to work well together when this amazing confluence all results in resonance. A dipole antenna hanging high between two trees will—on its design frequency and if properly constructed—present something close to 50 ohms impedance. Our typical coaxial feed line has a characteristic impedance of 50 ohms. The output circuit of your YaeKenElelcomTech radio craves a 50-ohm load.

There we are! Resonance! Maximum transfer of energy occurs! Music swells, flags unfurl, the sun breaks through the clouds, and all is right with the world! We have achieved resonance!

But then, relatively new ham radio operator, you simply cannot leave well enough alone. You go and do something dumb, like touch the tuning knob and change frequency up or down the band in search of new people with whom to chat. Or you go off down the band looking to chase some rare morsel of DX. Or, in a truly desperate move to find someone to talk with or to seek better propagation, you flip the switch to change to another amateur radio band entirely.

How dare you? Suddenly, your fancy, new transceiver is faced with an impedance value that is considerably removed from the Holy Grail of 50 ohms. The value may climb into the hundreds or even thousands of ohms, or drop to almost zero ohms of impedance, becoming disgustingly capacitively or inductively reactive. Suddenly, standing waves are introduced into the system as the RF energy encounters the ugliness of non-resonance. Energy is rudely rejected, deflected back down the coaxial feed line, all the way to the output of the transmitter from whence it came only a fraction of a second before, but it does not like the impedance it finds there either.

Zoom! Off it bounces once more, back up the cable, waving at its friends who are on their way back down already. But there are fewer and fewer of the reflected radio frequency waves now because some of them are being burned up—zapped energy—due to the loss in the coax.

Thankfully, if the carnage is too much—the standing waves now becoming too large a portion of the originally emitted energy—the transmitter does the only humane thing it can do. It shuts down to protect itself. Then it refuses to operate at that wavelength ever again.

You, dear operator, have no other choice. You return to the vicinity of the spot on the dial for which you originally designed that antenna, ignoring the limitless other frequencies and bands where others seem to play at will with no concern for the impedance encountered by their shiny YaeKenEleIcomTech radios.

But how do they do it? Gosh, there are ten amateur HF bands, and some of them are remarkably broad. Your transmitter only seems to like certain spots on those bands—those that are odd multiples of the design frequency of your nice dipole antenna, but those are few and far between and are mostly dead all the time. Yet others seem able to dance and frolic all across the spectrum, enjoying the full privilege of their licenses.

Finally, curiosity gets the best of you. You ask another ham when he wanders down to where you are stuck, in the middle of the band. He is on the air, operating all over the spectrum, even though his signal is not really all that strong when compared to some of the others. Still, he seems able to move and transmit even when he is farther away than a few kilohertz in either direction. Ah, glory! So you swallow your pride and ask him how he does it. Somehow, you manage to pull his answer out of the static and noise as he fades in and out.

"An antenna tuner!" he informs you. That is his secret.

Well, of course! All you need is that wonderful device that allows you to show your expensive radio a nice 50-ohm match and all is right with the world. You can dash and flip all over the RF spectrum, working everything you hear. You had no idea the answer was so simple! That box will contain the proper components for you to be able to load up all across the fruited plain! You grab the catalog or rush to the web site and place your order.

Soon the box arrives from the manufacturer and you hook the "tuner" up between the rig and the coax feed line, as instructed. You follow the directions and soon, after some spitting and sparking somewhere inside the radio as you learn to adjust the capacitor and inductor inside the shiny, new box, it shows you a wonderful thing on its sexy front-panel meter—a near one-to-one SWR! The rig's happy again. You go off to the hinterlands of each band, trying the thing out. It still balks in some places, but for the most part, it seems to load fine.

It should. The manufacturer's catalog said it would match almost any load. You have heard guys talk about loading to a bedspring, a hank of wire tossed out the window, a screen door.

And it cost two weeks' salary. It has to be good!

Soon you are able to transmit on frequencies previously unavailable to you, using your high-hung, well-designed, coax-fed dipole all over creation. Sometimes you actually get a response to people you call, though they often lose you before the QSO is completed. You even work DX, though the reports are typically bad, and you never seem to be able to get through in the pileups for the really rare ones. The microphone bites you when it touches your lip while you are talking. The XYL complains about the answering machine starting up by itself when you are on "that #%&*@ radio!" The neighbor lady stares at you angrily when you meet at the mailbox.

Hey, must be the sunspots. Propagation. The ionosphere sleeps most of the time, even though the web sites say there are plenty of sunspots. You only have a hundred watts. The bands are rife with static this time of the year. All ham stations have some RFI (radio frequency interference, usually to televisions and audio devices, it can raise its ugly head anywhere). The fact that your mic stings your lip confirms for you that the rig is making RF somewhere inside its box.

You vow you will do a better station ground someday, even though you thought you had a pretty good one already. At least you are on the air, exercising those new privileges, having a blast in the world's greatest hobby.

But there is still that nagging suspicion that other hams are hearing and getting out better than you are. It cannot be, though.

You have a one-to-one SWR. The meter says so. That is the best you can do, right? One-to-one? That means you have resonance, correct? Resonance! The rig is happy. You work DX sometimes. You get through on the local roundtable most of the time. And all with that one dipole, the only antenna you will be able to put up for a while.

Then, one day you have a nice conversation on a band far removed from your antenna's design frequency, talking with a distant station who has a really big signal. You assume he is running beau coups power, but when you ask what kind of amp he has, and that you've been considering getting one so you, too, can get out better, he tells you something that is hard to believe. Even though he has an amplifier, he does not even have the filaments turned on at the moment. He rarely uses the thing. Does not usually need to.

You grin. The guy's clearly lying. He is what you call "arm chair copy," one of the loudest signals on the band.

You ask about the antenna. He tells you it is a dipole, no higher or longer than yours. How about the tuner, then? Same make and model as yours. Lucky guy! He obviously lives in an RF hotspot, over great soil, maybe surrounded by saltwater. Nope. City lot. Rocky clay soil. Nearest saltwater is 500 miles away.

Then he casually mentions his feed line. It is something he calls "ladder line." 600-ohm ladder line, homebrew, using bits of plastic coat hanger cut to 6-inch lengths to keep parallel runs of 14-guage wire an equal distance apart as it runs from the antenna feed point to the house. It comes right into the shack, through a feed-through in a windowpane, directly to the balanced output of his "antenna matching device."

For some reason, he makes a point of not calling the box an "antenna tuner."

But what difference does this "ladder line" stuff make? You have some really nice RG-8X that the dealer said was perfectly fine for HF. And it is so easy to work with. "Ladder line" sounds ugly and not a little bit dangerous. And without a layer of copper shield to protect its insides, doesn't he have to be really careful where he runs the stuff to keep from frying neighborhood kids and small furry critters?

Then your new friend says he wants to tell you a few things about the old days so you will understand his preference for that old, outdated method of feeding RF to an antenna. You roll your eyes, check the station clock, and almost make up an excuse so you can tell him you have to QRT (quit transmitting and close your station). But it is still a few minutes until net time so you humor the guy and listen to what he is so darn anxious to tell you.

"Back in the early days of radio, hams had to find the easiest and most efficient ways of doing things," he tells you, his signal still making your S-meter tremble at the far right of its swing. "Often they had to make whatever part or device they needed. There was no coax cable back then. It had not yet been invented. They came up with air-dielectric feed line and found it worked very, very well. Nice, low loss. Cheap. Easy to make themselves. So the standard in those days was 600-ohm ladder line, two parallel runs of wire separated by some kind of non-conductive material every foot or so to make sure the distance between the two wires stayed about the same across its entire run from aerial to radio."

600 ohms? Your ears perk up. You are still learning about all this impedance stuff, but you know 600 ohms is a heck of a long way from the 50-ohm match your rig so desperately wants to see out its antenna connector. The 50 ohms your pretty run of coax presents. And a far cry from the impedance typically encountered at the feed point of a simple dipole antenna.

You ask him the "SWR" question. Surely it was a problem, even way back then, when dinosaurs roamed the earth and mastodons knocked down low-hung antennas.

"Back then, the output circuits of the tube-type rigs they used had a great deal of matching range built in," he explains. "Most of the inductors and capacitors we now find in our outboard antenna matching devices were a part of the transmitters way back in the early days. The capacitors and coils were built in. But even so, those guys not only didn't know much about standing waves, they didn't really worry much about it. The loss in that ladder line was so low, even if there was a mismatch at the antenna feed point, and even if there were standing waves on the line, the RF was eventually mostly all radiated. It did not get lost in the feed line, like it can in coax."

For some reason, you feel compelled to defend the honor of good, old coax. If ladder line was so good, why did everyone go to coax in the first place, once somebody built that better mousetrap?

"It is easy to use and work with, not a problem to run into a shack next to all kinds of other cables and metal, and the stuff works well in many instances," your new friend acknowledges. "For unbalanced antennas or VHF and UHF, it's preferable by far. Remember, though, that back in the day, there were no 60-, 30-, 17- or 12-meter bands yet. Most ops used a relatively narrow range of frequencies, and the typical antenna farm usually consisted of a dipole for 80/75, a dipole or vertical for 40, and a tri-band beam for 20, 15 and 10 meters. Nowadays, with so many potential operating frequencies, few of us can manage antennas that are specifically cut to work on each of those bands. Also, with today's transistorized radios and only a basic internal antenna matching device, even a broad-wavelength like 160 and 80/75 can cause problems with an antenna cut for either end if you want to operate at the opposite end. Thanks to the old-timers, we knew there was a way. And the way was the open-air-dielectric ladder line or mostly-open-air window line."

Net time has come and gone but you still do not get it. You ask him to clarify his position.

"Wait," you say, ignoring the tingle when the microphone brushes your lip. "You are saying SWR doesn't matter? That can't be!"

"Well, sure it matters, if it's a high enough mismatch. But by simply using a much lower loss feed line, you make SWR much less a factor. Look in the *ARRL Antenna Book* at the chart that shows the comparative loss between different types of coaxial cable and ladder or window line. There is loss in any real-world conductor, but it is so much less in the old-fashioned stuff that it makes those trips up and down the feed line for reflected power much easier, and most of it gets radiated eventually by your antenna, not burned up in your coaxial cable."

But what about that 600-to-50-ohm mismatch back at the rig? 12 to 1 SWR? Serious stuff! Your radio ain't gonna like that one bit!

"Best thing for a balanced, ladder-line-fed antenna system is what is called a balanced antenna matching unit, which is, of course, designed for matching a balanced antenna system. It does a nice, effective job of matching the 50-ohm output of your rig to whatever impedance you encounter. And believe me, that impedance will vary all over the place when you try to use one big dipole on all ten bands. But it is not really a worry. The low-loss line takes care of most load mismatches you'll see. Those standing waves eventually go dancing off into space to hopefully be reflected back to earth somewhere near that big DXpedition everybody's calling."

You check to make sure but you have a balanced output on your tuner...er...antenna matching device. Can't you just use that to match the antenna?

"Sure," he says. "That's what I'm doing right now, though I'm going to build myself a balanced tuner when I get the time and find the parts I need. It's an easy project, even for a beginner. You and I have a 4-to-1 current-type balun...a balanced-to-unbalanced transformer...in the ATU...antenna tuning unit, if you want to call it that...and the circuit inside the device will present a nominal 50-ohm load to your transmitter. Our balun is heavy enough to work fine at the power levels we use, but I have another much heftier unit I use when I throw on the afterburner. Some ATUs use voltage-type baluns or they simply are not built tough enough to handle the kinds of mismatches you may encounter on a very wide range of frequencies you might want to operate on. Those don't give very good results and could even fail. By the way, I don't call them `antenna tuners' for a reason. You are not `tuning' the `antenna.' The typical way most folks `tune' a dipole antenna is make it longer or shorter, or higher or lower in relationship to the ground beneath it. What you are really doing with that box in the shack is matching your transmitter to the antenna system. It is an antenna *system*!"

How can you tell if the internal balun isn't "tough enough?" you ask.

"Smoke and flames," he says and laughs. "Just make sure the thing is rated for much higher power than what you intend to run. By the way, there are other ways to do this thing, you know. Want to hear about them?"

You ignore the XYL (wife) screaming about your "Donald Duck voice" messing up *American Idol* on her TV set and tell him to go ahead.

There are some logistical problems with open wire line, he admits. It needs to be kept at least a few inches away from other metal, cables, and the ground. He tells you about how some hams run the ladder line to a balun outside the shack and use as short a run of high-quality, low loss coax as they need to get inside the house and to the tuner. They usually have a one-to-one balun for this purpose since it's typically best to pass whatever impedance you encounter at the feed point to the tuner. If your system sees a very low impedance, you do not want to step it down any more. Matching devices do better when they are attempting to match higher impedances rather than lower ones.

Some fellows put a balun right there at the feed point, then run coax to the shack. That is not necessarily a good idea for an antenna you plan to use on multiple bands (it IS a good idea if your dipole will only be used on one band or odd multiples of its resonant frequency). That is because there will still be standing waves as you move around the bands and they will still be dissipated as heat in the coax cable.

There are some who put a remote matching device at the feed point, tuning for 50 ohms, and then running coax. That works pretty well, but you still have to have an ATU that can stand weather, be light enough that it does not drag down your aerial, and has current running to it so you can remotely change the capacitive and inductive parameters from your operating position in order to find the best match.

Other hams tape two runs of good, low-loss 50-ohm coax together and solder each of the two sides of the ladder line to the center conductors of the coax cables. Then the grounds are tied together on the matching device end and hooked to the station ground. Finally, the two center conductors are attached to the balanced output of the matching device. The twin-run of coax should be kept as short as possible, of course, but the 100-ohm impedance presented is little or no problem.

You think for a moment. You have saved your best question for last. You ignore the buzzing sound from your nearby computer speakers as you speak into the microphone.

"But regardless of the feed line, using an antenna on frequencies where it is nowhere near resonant is not as good as having an antenna cut to resonance for that frequency, right? This is just a compromise and we pay a heavy price for trying to use just one antenna from 1.8 to 30 megahertz."

So you have said it. A cut-to-resonant-length antenna is always better. There is only a slight pause on the other end of the circuit as your new buddy frames his response.

"You've been listening to some of the guys on 75 meters, right? Or reading those forums on the Internet. First thing, don't think of it as an 'antenna.' Think of it as an 'antenna system.' There are lots of things that make up your antenna system—the output circuit of your transmitter, the cable to the ATU, the ATU, the feed line to the antenna, the antenna itself, the earth beneath it, the trees in your yard, the chain link fence at the back of the lot, a mountain a mile away, the atmosphere above you. Obviously you don't have much control over some of that. Over *most* of that. But you can bring a good portion of it into a state that is what we call 'resonance.' You have two goals in the process.

"First, because of the way most of our solid-state radios are designed to work these days, you must present a load at the output of the rig that is relatively close to 50 ohms. Some radios are more forgiving than others, but a serious mismatch will either damage the rig or cause it to cut back power or shut off completely. Most amplifiers—and especially the new solid state ones—are just as picky about the load they prefer. If the mismatch is so great that the rig won't work, it's darn hard to make contacts!

"Your second goal in life is to cause the antenna...the wire-in-the-sky part of the system...to radiate as much of the power that you send it as it can. Yes, one way to do that is to trim the antenna so that it is non-reactive at a particular frequency—the one you use all the time—and close to 50 ohms. Then you can feed it with coax. Even then, you may want a balun at the feed point to try to keep common mode currents off the shield of the coax and stray RF out of the shack and house. That RF energy does you no good there. It just makes XYLs and neighbors really irritable and gives you a painful tingle sometimes. But remember, the farther you venture from the design frequency of the antenna, the greater the mismatch, and eventually, with coax, the standing waves will be high enough to cause loss of precious power. Yes, the antenna will work okay at odd multiples of the lowest design frequency, but how many of those actually fall within an amateur band? And yes, you may be able to dial in the right combination of inductive and capacitive reactance to please your radio, but you won't be throwing much of your original power in the direction of the DX station's antenna system. It is going to be running up and down your coax cable until it gets dissipated...burned up...as heat."

He offers to email you a diagram of the antenna system he built when he first began to experiment with the old hams' way of doing things. He promises it is cheap and simple, and that the dipole part of the antenna system is decidedly non-resonant—by itself—at an almost infinite number of frequencies. It is not even the best setup possible, he notes, but it is far better than what you are currently using. It is cut to be a total of a half-wavelength long (each leg is a quarter-wavelength and should be exactly the same length so it will be truly balanced) for the lowest frequency that is anticipated to be used...or that will fit in a yard. He maintains that it would work fine on most bands from there through ten meters when used with ladder line or window line, 300 to 600 ohm impedance, and a good quality one-to-one balun.

After saying your 73 ("best regards"), you sit back and think about what the nice mentor has said. It does make sense. So much so that you invest in an antenna book and do some research on the web. Though you still see some of the "resonant antennas are the be-all, end-all" posts and hear on the air lots of people preaching the gospel of the resonant antenna, you also see lots of information that backs up what the fellow has told you.

You Google "W2DU" and read excerpts from his book on the subject. You visit W4RNL's web site and find a wealth of information. You purchase a good-quality one-to-one current-type balun, a spool of inexpensive window line, and a good, strain-relief center insulator designed for the open-air-dielectric feed line. Then, when you get the antenna built and up in the air, you marvel at what you have been missing all this time.

And you vow that from now on, you will begin listening to what the old folks say. Sometimes, while they were dodging dinosaurs and mastodons and discovering fire, they actually figured out how to make simple antennas work much better!

Chapter 8 -- The Antenna Party

Everybody says it so it must be true. The performance of a homebrew antenna is directly proportional to how rotten the weather is when it is installed.

That was one reason why we had high hopes for young Jack Oakley's aerial that hot, summer day. Several of us had gathered early, while it was merely sweltering and not yet hellish hot, as it would be in only a few hours. We came equipped with tools, rope, wire, insulators, a balun, feedline, a short section of coax, a slingshot and a fishing reel—all we needed to build a proper multi-band dipole antenna.

Jack met us at the door, excited, greeting us with a string of thank-yous as he shook each of our hands. He motioned for us to follow him through the small, dark house and out onto the patio behind. There, he had a tub waiting, filled with ice, sodas, and beer.

"Aw, Jack, you didn't have to do that," I told him, but that did not prevent us from reaching in and grabbing ourselves some cold drinks.

"You guys didn't have to give up your Saturday to come do this, either. What can I do to help?"

"I think you just did," Win McCullers, our ace-slingshot-shooter told him after a big swig. As he took another slug, he was already eyeing some high tree limbs on the tall elms that lined the back of Jack's small lot. He winked at the rest of us, then headed off toward the far corner of Jack's backyard.

"How high you reckon you can get it?" Jack asked.

"High as it needs to be," I told him. "We'll cut it for the low end of 80...you still want to do some CW down there, don't you?...and if I know Win, he may hook one end of it to the moon and the other one to Mars."

"Are you sure you have enough room?" Jack asked. "I don't think my lot is big enough for...what?...a hundred and thirty-five feet?"

"We'll make it work," I told him. "Win is an expert at lot stretching. I once saw him fit a rhombic into a phone booth."

Jack had an odd look on his face. I did not know if he was unfamiliar with the term "rhombic" or "phone booth." Kids! Well, he was somewhere in his early twenties and that certainly made him a "kid" to me.

Meanwhile, Grady Harrison was unspooling the flexweave copper wire, taking one end toward the other side of the yard.

"You guys going to stand there and tell lies or you going to bring one end of the tape measure over here?" Grady asked, employing his usual gruff-old-grouch demeanor. "I don't know for certain, but I suspect it will get hot here directly."

I tapped Jack on the shoulder, told him thanks again for the drink, grabbed the 100-foot tape, and headed that way. Win was already about to launch a lead weight attached to s spool of fishing line, his slingshot aimed for a nice, horizontal limb about fifty feet from the ground. He had painted the weight a brilliant yellow, and I could easily follow its arc as it flew perfectly over the limb and disappeared behind the leaves on the other side.

"First time!" Win whooped. "Sometimes I amaze myself."

"Even a blind pig finds an acorn," Grady started but hushed immediately as he tied off the end of the antenna wire to a bush. "Here, give me the tape and see if you can remember your numbers long enough to take it yonder way sixty-seven-feet-six-inches."

"You sure you have the strength to hold onto it, there, Grady?" I jibed. "I know how weak you old folks get if you miss your daily dose of Geritol."

As soon as I marked the spot with a piece of electrical tape, Grady quickly wrapped his end of the antenna wire around a ceramic "egg" insulator.

"Measure it again, just to make sure," he told me. "I'd hate to have to un-cut it if you get it too short." But the wire was right on the money. I pulled a pair of wire cutters from my pocket and clipped it a few inches past my mark. Grady handed me a commercially made center insulator, designed to keep strain off the ladder line that we planned to use for a feedline. While I attached the one leg of the antenna to the center insulator, Grady fussed.

"I can't believe it. Time was, we would have made that insulator out of a chunk of Plexiglas or whatever we could find in the junk box instead of going out and buying a contraption like that," he grumbled.

"Yeah, then you would get the opportunity to replace it with some other piece of jury-rigged junk the first time a bird lit on the thing." I had learned a long time ago that Grady Harrison loved to argue and complain almost as much as he loved cobbling together tube-type amplifiers and jawing with his buddies on the air. He was of the opinion that nothing good had happened in electronics and radio since 1952. And anybody unfortunate enough to not have been around or in the hobby of ham radio before that could not be a part of his fraternity.

Grady was a decent enough guy. His presence this blistering hot day to help a young ham who needed it was proof enough of that. But sometimes his curmudgeon act wore a bit thin. Especially as the temperature and humidity rose ever higher and the chiggers came out for brunch.

I felt a tug on the half-built antenna. Win was already tying a piece of strong, UV-resistant rope to the end insulator, ready to draw it end over the tree limb when the time came.

"Reckon you can make another piece of wire exactly as long as this one without doing any damage?" Grady asked me.

"I can get it close."

"If we just wanted 'close' I could have left my tape measure at the house. You want a balanced antenna. That means both sides are the same length. Balanced."

"Really? Grady, I don't know what I would do without you?"

I caught a glimpse of Jack Oakley. He had moved his wheelchair a few feet to get into a patch of shade on the patio.

"You got the transceiver warmed up?" I called to him. "We'll be working DX in a few minutes."

"It's all solid state. I didn't think you had to warm those up."

"Humph!" Grady said, just loud enough for only me to hear him. "Where do they get their licenses these days? Out of cornflake boxes?"

"Grady, that kid..." I started, but Win was there, butane torch in hand. He also had a bundle of coiled-up ladder line.

We made quick work of punching a hole in the middle of the line and attaching it to the center insulator with a nylon screw and nut, and then we wrapped each of the two feedline conductors around the opposing legs of the dipole. Being careful not to get the wires too hot or melt the insulator, Win soldered everything together, allowed it to cool, then pulled hard in every direction. We had good connections all around, but Grady insisted on pulling out his volt-ohm meter and checking continuity all the way to the far end of each leg of the aerial and to the end of the ladder line.

It was really getting hot as we watched Win step off the distance to a tree in the front corner of Jack's lot. He then looked up and considered the various branches above him.

"Just enough," he announced. "We won't have to make this thing an ugly 'Z' after all."

It took him several tries to get his fishing line and sinker over this limb since he had to avoid any chance of shooting it as far as a power line across the street or have his brightly colored weight go through the neighbor's picture window. A group of neighborhood kids had gathered on the sidewalk, too, and he did not want to bean one of them.

There is no correlation that I could remember between blood, concussions, and antenna performance.

"It'll never fit," Grady firmly announced. He had been eyeballing the distance between the two trees at the corners of Jack's lot. "Ain't far enough between them trees."

"Grady, you are about the most optimistic fellow I think I have ever encountered," I told him sarcastically. He really was beginning to irritate me.

Win simply winked at me, grinned, pulled his rope over the limb, and tied it snugly onto the other egg insulator.

"Go pull the other end up so the insulator is a couple of feet from the limb," he told me. I did. Grady just stood there in the middle, shaking his head before stomping off. The feedline, hooked to the center of the antenna, uncoiled as the insulator rose into the air. Then Win pulled the rope on his end. Sure enough, when we pulled the wire reasonably taut, he had about three feet between his insulator and the limb. The antenna just fit, as if those trees had been planted in those exact spots just for supporting an 80-meter dipole antenna.

"Benevolent vegetation," Win called it.

Grady was not paying any attention to us, though. Proven wrong, he was now on a stepladder, grumbling the entire time, attaching a small, enclosed balun to the underside of an eave on the house, just above the window to Jack's den. He checked a marking on the ladder line, cut it there, and hooked it to the balanced side of the balun. His grumbling grew even louder as he screwed the connector on the end of a short piece of coax to the other side and then stuck it beneath the screen, poked beneath the narrow opening where the window was barely raised, and fed it inside.

"Don't tell anybody you just saw me doing this," he said to Jack. "It would surely ruin my reputation. Baluns? Ladderline?

Automatic antenna tuners? No wonder nobody can hear most of these guys on the bands these days, unless they're runnin' a California kilowatt."

Win and I tried to ignore Grady's grousing. He was still convinced every radio should have tubes and anything between the output of the radio and the feed point of the antenna—anything besides open wire feedline—was an atrocity. Anybody caught using such should have to turn his license back in to the FCC.

We quickly surveyed our work. The antenna was stretched from one convenient tree to another, high above the yard from one extreme corner to the opposite one. The ladder line fell straight down from its middle for forty feet or so before it stretched over to the balun Grady had reluctantly hung beneath the eave. We had tied off both end ropes for the time being and would come back and use opposing 8-penny nails driven into the tree trunks as cleats to do a more permanent securing. We would install a spring on one end to take the tension if a strong wind decided to blow the two trees in opposite directions.

"All right, let's see how she plays," Win said.

Jack was already inside with the radio on. Grady followed with the toolbox and the volt-ohm meter. We stopped long enough to grab drinks and went inside. The air conditioning felt wonderful.

Win twisted the coax onto the connector on the back of the automatic antenna-matching device on Jack's desk, then made sure the other jumper led from the HF antenna connection on the transceiver to the input of the tuner and that all connectors were screwed on tightly.

"Ready to go, Jack," Win announced. "See if she works."

Jack pushed a button on a small box that rested on the desk in front of his radio.

"Three point eight three zero," said a tinny, mechanical voice. Jack spun the dial on the rig and hit the button on the box again. "Three point five one five."

He felt for the button on the front of the automatic tuner and punched. Relays chattered inside the device and the cross-needles on the dial swayed rhythmically up and down. Win and I looked at each other as the box rattled away for a good ten seconds. Then it sent "di di dit" and waved the two needles in surrender.

The SWR was too high. The matching device could not tune it.

"Hmmm," was all Win could manage.

"It's all that computerized stuff and that dang balun," Grady said from the back of the room. "Told you. I got some coils and a capacitor in my junk box and we could breadboard up a quick tuner that would match the radio to a butter knife."

"And have as much loss as a ten-foot two-by-four and enough stray RF to cook supper, too," Win told him, taking a long draw from his bottle of soda as he considered this disappointing development. "Besides, it might be a hassle for Jack to have to mess with a Rube Goldberg apparatus like that."

I tried to ignore the look of disappointment on Jack's face as I turned to address our official club curmudgeon.

"Grady, we got some other problem going on here and we'll figure out what it is and get some fire in the wire for old Jack, here," I told him, mostly for Jack's benefit. What with the humidity and heat and the trouble with the antenna, Grady was really beginning to grate on my nerves. But I held my tongue.

"Most likely that store-bought balun. We could have left that out altogether if he didn't have that rice box for a radio."

Win was gazing out the window, studying the antenna, its center conductor high in the air, swaying just slightly in the breeze. The feedline came down perfectly to the terminals on the balun and the short run of coax fed—without being pinched beneath the window—to the tuner output.

"Let's see," Win said. "Let's do this logically. We measured twice and cut once, right? Even so, a few inches would not make that much difference. And we checked continuity at the feed point, too?"

"I did," Grady confirmed.

"And the feed line?"

"It's okay...for that dang ladder line stuff, anyway."

"No reason to suspect a problem with the balun, Grady. It was working fine last time I used it."

"Baluns. Hummmph!"

"Jack's been using his tuner on that little short loop of his and it has worked okay in places on the band. No reason to suspect it has gone south on us."

"Tuner? That ain't nothing but a bunch of micro-processors and relays!" Grady spat out "micro-processors" as if it was a dirty word.

Win was scratching his chin. So was I. There just was not much that could have gone wrong. The antenna was about as simple as they come. I was about to start wondering if maybe Grady was right about the balun or tuner being on the fritz.

"Did we check the coax?" Jack suddenly piped up. "That seems to be the only thing we haven't looked at. I think the jumper from the rig to the tuner is okay. At least it was working last night when I used it."

Grady looked at Jack as if to say, Rookie, what do you know?

"Naw! Can't be the other run of coax. I built that up myself last night," Grady said.

"Did you check it after you put the connectors on it?" Win asked.

"I didn't have to. I've been soldering coax connectors since 1951. Ain't never had one fail yet."

"Just for giggles and grins, let me see your meter, Mr. Marconi," Win told him.

Grady shook his head as he handed the volt-ohm meter over to Win. I unscrewed the coax from the back of the auto-tuner and gave it to him. He touched one probe to the outside of the connector and the other to the center pin. The meter flew over to the right-hand peg.

"Shorted," Win reported for Jack's benefit. Grady and I could see it for ourselves. "Dead short."

"It's that dang balun. I told you. Something's shorted inside that thing."

"Okay, go take the other end loose, then," Win told him, but Grady was already headed out the backdoor, anxious to show us the error of our ways. He climbed back up on the ladder and unscrewed the cable from the balun's SO-239 connector.

Again, Win touched the two sides of the coax. The volt-ohm meter's indicator once more flew to the right. Win turned to me and grinned. We could hear Grady snorting through the window. He saw the glee on our faces.

"Let me guess," Jack said, flashing his own broad smile. "It's the coax that's bad."

"Yes sir," Win confirmed for him. "The Coax King out there either grabbed a bad piece of cable or shorted something when he put on one of the connectors. Most hams would have at least checked it once they got it built. Reckon we ought to make him turn in his license to the FCC?"

"No!" Jack said. "He didn't…"

"Just kidding," Win told him. "But it is kind of sweet to see him get his come-uppance once in a while."

"Look, I have another jumper over there under the table," Jack said. "It's RG-8X. I was going to use it from the rig to the solid-state amp when I get it."

"Don't let the old man hear you say 'solid state' and 'amp' in the same sentence!" I told Jack. "He'll have a stroke right there on your patio." We all three laughed.

We quickly handed one end of the new cable out to Grady and screwed the other onto the tuner. Again Jack touched the transceiver's "Tune" button. Again the box chattered, but this time only a couple of quick clicks. The digital readout on the device said "1 : 1." So did the tinny voice from the little box on the desk.

We looked on as Jack moved up the band and tried tuning up in several spots. The automatic tuner made quick work of it.

Then he tried several other bands. Though it took longer to find a match in a couple of places, it still managed it just fine. We could also hear some very strong signals and occasional bursts of static.

Then, on the low end of 20 meters, a station on an island off the eastern coast of Africa was working a writhing, boisterous pileup with hundreds of stations calling him. Jack used his sense of touch to flip the mode switch to CW and to synch up and then split the radio's VFOs.

"Reckon I ought to give him a try?" he asked.

"Why not?" Win and I told him in unison.

All the while, Grady sat in the back corner of the room, intently studying the short piece of coax as if he had never seen such a thing before. As if he could spot the electrical short in the bad cable just by staring at it.

When the DX station paused to listen again, Jack sucked in a deep breath and sent his call with the old paddle he used. The station answered and quickly worked someone else.

Again, Jack sent his call letters. Nope. Another station.

Jack shrugged.

"Oh, well. Maybe I'll see how the antenna tunes up on 17," he suggested.

"Hey, don't give up so easy," I told him. "He's got a good signal, and I'll bet he isn't running any more power or any better antenna than you are."

He breathed deeply again and sent his call sign one more time.

Silence.

Then Jack's call letters, coming back from the other side of the world, followed with "599."

For a moment, I thought Jack might be so shocked that he would not even be able to respond. The young ham's hand was shaking so badly he could hardly answer, but he managed his own "599 TU 73," even with his trembling keying hand.

"TU 73," came the response.

Jack Oakley's dark glasses were slightly askew on his nose when he spun around in our direction, but the broad smile on his face told us all we needed to know.

"I got him! I got him!"

He quickly typed out the call letters and signal reports on his Braille keyboard. Then, he turned right back to the radio and began twisting the dial, eagerly searching for more signals, more worlds to conquer and communicate with.

Meanwhile, Grady sat there watching the whole thing, a sheepish expression behind his full beard.

"Who'd he call? Did he copy him?"

"Grady, you really ought to learn CW when you get the chance," I told him.

"I learned it. I learned it enough to get my General Class license way back when. Ain't touched a key since. Never seen a need. That stuff is so old-fashioned."

Win and I looked at each other and grinned. Meanwhile, Jack had pounced on an SM5 (a station in Sweden) and was already exchanging signal reports.

As we headed outside, we grabbed yet another soda from the ice in the tub. We needed to secure the ends of that fine antenna before a thunderstorm blew up. Then we would help Jack locate the connection on the back of the tuner so he would be able to unscrew it and drop it outside for lightning protection.

A nice breeze had sprung up and somehow, it did not seem nearly as hot and humid as it had only a few moments before.

I do not want to belabor the point. However, the subject of resonance in an antenna system is one that will not go away. It is also central to understanding how antenna systems actually work and how any amateur radio operator can get the most out of whatever antenna system he or she is able to put up.

So, let us revisit the subject and spend just a little more time on its intricacies, and how you can use what you learn to make your station better.

Oh, and it could help you hold your own in some interesting discussions.

Chapter 9 -- Resonance Schmesonance!

I am not trying to get a war started. All I am really trying to do is help others in our hobby—not just newcomers—understand one of the basic concepts of radio frequency transmission: antenna system resonance. Understand it and use it to their benefit so they may better enjoy our wonderful hobby.

There, I said it. RESONANCE. Notice, though, that I used the phrase antenna system resonance. I know of no one using only an "antenna" to send electromagnetic waves whirling off into the sky. They likely have much more between the output stage of their final amplifier (not just a "kicker" but the amplifier inside your radio as well) and the ionosphere. Much more than just what we typically refer to as an "antenna." And all that stuff in the chain affects that fleeting mystery ingredient we call "resonance."

(By the way, if you ever see anyone writing about a "resonate antenna" be sure to promptly flail him or her with a length of old left-over RG-59 coax! "Resonate" is a verb. "Resonant" is an adjective.)

Let me start with a strong statement: achieving a perfectly resonant antenna system is virtually impossible. By "antenna," I mean a transducer—a thingy that changes one form of energy into another, and for our purposes, we'll call it an antenna (but I really mean an "antenna system"). It is part of an electrical circuit that changes AC current into electromagnetic waves. The system at resonance forms a more-or-less tuned circuit, which throws in equal doses of inductive reactance and capacitive reactance. At resonance, they cancel each other out, leaving only resistance. And I am talking two kinds of resistance: loss and radiation. For the purposes of this little conversation starter, let's ignore loss—which is not usually a big factor at HF frequencies—and concentrate on the good stuff...radiation resistance, something we all want to conjure up as much of as we can.

Now, ponder for a moment all the possible variations of capacitive and inductive reactance that might be swirling around from the rear end of your radio, the jumper to the above-mentioned "kicker," all the guts inside the amp, the jumper to the antenna matching device (I'm philosophically opposed to the term "antenna tuner" because you are NOT tuning the antenna with that box at all!), the innards of the "tuner," your watt meter and the cables into and out of it, the feedline, the hank of wire or aluminum that we call an "antenna," all the various connectors and insulators and maybe even a balun, your kid's swing set, the neighbor's metal-roofed garage, and even the sunspot-influenced stuff God put up in the sky above you. Gosh, even the dirt in your yard enters into the equation. And your neighbor's yard. And all the way beyond the horizon. All part of your antenna "system!"

My, my, my. Hard to imagine it would ever be possible to bring those two forces of reactance to a point where they perfectly cancel each other out and allow every microwatt of power from your little transmitter to shoot off your antenna, launched in the direction of that highly-prized DXpedition or that net you want to check into. But it can happen. Not very easily. But, technically, it can happen.

That is one of the things you bought that matching device for in the first place. You can make it appear to your radio that you have that perfect resonance out there in the back yard, stretched between two shade trees or clamped to a mast on top of the tower. With those controls on the front of the matchbox, you can adjust its internal components, thus presenting to your transmitter the exact value of impedance—the two reactances canceling each other out—that the rig wants to see. (I know. The matching device can go out there closer to the feed point, too, and would work better in many situations, but that is beyond the scope of this conversation starter.)

Just for grins, let us say Jupiter aligns with Mars and you happen to cut the antenna perfectly, have precisely the correct length of feedline, the ground and earthworms in it present the right amount of conductivity, and Junior's swing set is exactly the correct distance from the antenna feed point. Capacitive and inductive reactance balance beautifully, wiping each other out, leaving only the good stuff: delightful radiation resistance.

Whooppee! You have achieved a resonant antenna system! The much-worshipped standing wave ratio is 1:1. You are emitting about as much of your precious RF into space as you possibly could manage, based on the immutable laws of physics.

Then you go and do something dumb, like QSY (change frequencies) up or down the band a couple of hundred kilocycles, chasing a DX station or to find a clear spot to talk with a buddy.

Aw, heck! The aerial is no longer resonant.

Either Mr. Capacitive or Mr. Inductive have the upper hand. The needle on the SWR meter sways disturbingly upward. Impedance dips toward zero ohms or zooms toward the sky, abandoning "50 ohms" completely. You begin worrying about your considerable investment in your nice radio.

Aw, in truth it is probably no big deal on 40 meters or lower wavelengths. A dipole cut for the middle of the band on 40 or above will probably still work okay from one end to the other. But it will not be resonant. No, it won't.

Heaven forbid you try to use that dipole on some other band that is not an odd harmonic of the one for which you cut it. Resonant? Not by a long shot then. And maybe so far off that your radio spits and sparks.

Oh, you might be able to adjust that matchbox so the radio is fine with everything. But signals suddenly seem weaker. People ignore you when you call them. You scream and squawk but the DX stations no longer seem to hear you. The radio thinks there is a resonant aerial out there in the backyard, but you and the RF gods soon know different.

"But wait, OM," you say. "You told us resonance did not matter. Were you trying to get a fight started after all?"

Well, I did say that, and maybe I should have clarified it a bit. Within reason, resonance is not necessary to communicate with relative effectiveness. The men who went to the moon used decidedly non-resonant antennas in their radio communications. Few AM broadcast stations have truly resonant antennas. They use capacitors and coils—sound like that "antenna tuner" on your desk?—to get a match to their towers (which, for AM broadcasters, are their antennas).

Only thing is, once those AM broadcasters start transmitting on their assigned frequency and have everything set, they do not have to change anything. As opposed to you, you QSYing, band-hopping fool, you. That is, they do not have to adjust anything until something else changes, like the ground system starts to deteriorate.

So why do we work so hard to make resonant antenna systems if it does not really matter all that much?

It actually does, in some cases. Even if you can get your matchbox to present a lovely 50-ohm load through your coaxial cable and into whatever your antenna system might be, it will not be nearly as efficient a radiator as a dipole cut to frequency.

If you use a feedline that has higher loss when presented with standing waves, then you would want your antenna to be a lot closer to resonance. Again, that is true, even if your lovely antenna matching device seems to have all that mess worked out. Handy and pretty as coax cable is, it will not work nearly as well if presented with a load that is way off from 50 ohms of impedance.

There are alternatives. As previously discussed, open-air-dielectric feedline is the best. Or window line. It is cheap, virtually ignores standing waves, and allows you to use one non-resonant-in-most-places antenna across a broad part of the radio spectrum. It has its quirks, too, I'll grant you, and we have discussed those already.

So here is what I am saying:

1. It is very difficult to achieve perfect resonance in an antenna system, but it can be done.

2. But is it really worth it?

3. If you do devise a resonant antenna system, once you venture up or down the band a ways, or you jump to another band entirely, you are moving farther and farther from Shangri La. Results may deteriorate rapidly.

4. An antenna matching device can allow you to use a very, very non-resonant antenna system, but the result may or may not be a good one.

5. With the proper circuitry (antenna matching components) and a feedline that is not a stickler for resonance, you can still use a very, very non-resonant antenna with very, very good results.

6. Learn more about SWR and resonance so you do not become a slave to them, but so you can manage them in such a way that you get the results you want.

Look, maybe you are one of those guys or gals who camps on one frequency on one band all day every day. Fine. Get that dang antenna as close to resonance as you can. Do not invest in a matching device. Feed it with coax. And knock yourself out. Brag that you don't believe in "antenna tuners." "I only use resonant antennas!" you expound. Good for you, Chief. Enjoy that narrow little sliver of spectrum while the rest of us flit about across a broad swath of the shortwaves, chewing rags and nailing DX.

See, we want to get a taste of every cycle of spectrum we have available to us. Few of us are able to put up a couple of dozen "resonant" antennas to do so. (To be fair, with a decent multi-band antenna like a hexbeam or fan dipole and enough dipoles to cover 160 through 30, I figure you could get by with six or seven antennas without being too far off resonance. A trap vertical could probably cover 160 through 10, but it will not be resonant in many places on some of those longer wavelengths! Some guys even sell multi-band, no-radials-required verticals, but good luck filling your logbook using one of those.)

Fact is, many of us prefer not spending all our operating time worrying about "resonance." Or fidgeting about standing waves. Wringing our hands as we glare at the SWR meter.

We would much rather learn how to manage these things, take advantage of the science, and apply it so we can have a perfectly wonderful experience every time we throw the "ON" switch.

Besides, learning and experimenting with this stuff is where a lot of the fun happens anyway.

Chapter 10 -- Feeding the Beast—Transferring Radio Frequency Energy from Your Transmitter to Your Antenna

If you are not tired of antennas and feed lines and such already, let us—with apologizes to Mr. William Shakespeare—spend just a few more words talking about "feeding the beast," or getting maximum transfer of power from transmitter to ether.

We continue to have an influx of relatively new operators to the HF amateur radio bands as more and more people recognize the attraction of the hobby. These newcomers may or may not have experience with or knowledge of the compromises involved with building antenna systems. They may try to get by cheaply and quickly, just to get a taste of the new spectrum now available to them. And in the process, they may have a less than satisfying experience.

In this chapter, I will not attempt to even delve into the antennas themselves. There are myriad choices for information, including books like the oft-mentioned *ARRL Antenna Handbook* and in discussion forums on sites like eHam.net and QRZ.com. I would recommend to any newcomer that he or she learn along the way but keep it simple in the beginning.

By all means, once you are legal and have obtained your license and call letters, get an antenna up so you can be on the air, joining in on the fun! But for the time being, avoid phased arrays, delta loops, and exotic hunks of metal in the sky. For the moment, stick with dipoles, verticals, or simple loops, as we have already discussed. They are easier to play with and you might learn something from installing them. If you purchase commercially made antennas, be sure to follow the manufacturer's directions closely, including recommendations for properly getting the RF from your radio/amplifier to the antenna itself.

We will talk about expanding beyond that "get on the air" antenna in the next chapter. But right now, we will discuss feeding your antenna. There are several potential combinations of feed systems and matching units that are commonly used by amateurs. For our purposes, we will consider the following simpler and more typical ones:

--Coaxial cable with no matching unit except what might be internal to the transmitter

--Coaxial cable with an external outboard matching unit

--Open wire or ladder line with or without an external outboard matching unit

Wait, what is this "matching unit" stuff? You mean a "tuner?"

Actually, an antenna tuner is a matching unit, and one quite often employed by hams, but there are other means and devices for matching rigs to antennas that are not "tuners." These devices are technically a part of the antenna system, as you have learned already. Matching units allow the operator to vary the capacitive and inductive reactance seen by the transmitter in order to get a better "match," to allow as much of the radio frequency energy coming from the transmitter to be transferred to the antenna and into the air as possible.

Let us talk "matching" for a moment. Most transmitters and outboard amplifiers today are designed to work best when they are outputting radio frequency into an impedance of 50 ohms. The operator has very little control over the load impedance of the typical transistorized transceiver today—except with its built-in auto-tuner, found in most modern radios—and not much more control over the output impedance matching of a common amplifier. However, the impedance presented by different antennas at different frequencies can vary widely and the operator may need to dramatically vary the reactance values the transmitter encounters in order to try to get a better transfer of power to the feed line first, and possibly to the antenna itself. There are other matching devices, such as baluns, mechanical devices like so-called gamma matches at the antenna feed point, and even relays that switch in and out all sorts of odd components in a Rube Goldberg-type setup.

For the purpose of this article, let's consider the matching unit to be either an antenna matching device internal to your radio or a similar external device, either of which is typically called an "antenna tuner."

Coaxial cable, or simply "coax," is a very popular means of getting radio frequency energy from transceiver to antenna, and vice versa for receiving, of course. The more popular types are already designed to offer 50 ohms impedance (or relatively close), are easy to work with, can be run in close proximity to other cables, tower legs, or metal objects, and use simple connectors that can be securely attached to the transmitter and the antenna. Coax is a good choice for an antenna such as a dipole that is designed to be used on only one operating band (or odd multiple harmonics of that band). It also works well with beam-type antennas and on VHF and UHF frequencies. Such an antenna, properly constructed and cut close to the preferred operating frequency so as to be in resonance, will show impedance close enough to 50 ohms. Your feedline and your transmitter output circuit will be happy and everything will be in harmony. The maximum amount of energy possible will be moved from transmitter to feed line to antenna and emitted into space.

But what about very broad amateur bands, like 15 meters, or those bands that require more antenna-per-hertz because of the long, long wavelength, like 160 meters? It is asking a lot of a piece of wire and its feedline to be close to resonant across such a wide band. Even if the wire is cut for the middle of the band, it may be considerably out of resonance—offering impedance that is a long way removed from 50 ohms—when you try to use it at the extreme ends of the band. This creates the phenomenon we call "standing waves." Simply put, standing waves are currents that are reflected—due to a mismatch—back from the feed point of the antenna, returning back down the feedline toward the transmitter. SWR—or "standing wave ratio"—is a way of expressing the amount of your outgoing power that is getting reflected back down the feedline. (This is a rather simplistic description of a decidedly complicated thing that is going on, but I believe it is accurate and will suffice for this discussion.)

Let me state here that achieving a low SWR is mostly a good thing, though not an absolutely critical one. But I thought high SWR was evil incarnate! Isn't all that power that gets sent back in the direction of the shack wasted? And isn't it wasted in the form of heat? Am I not required to get no worse than a 1-to-1 match? Well, the RF energy does not necessarily go back into your radio or get burned up. A portion of it is simply sent right back up the feedline each time it is reflected. If the feedline has relatively low loss, you really do not lose much of the RF at all. Most of it is eventually sent out into the ether by the antenna. The fact that some of it made a lot of trips up and down the feedline before it was emitted into space is immaterial. Granted, a very large SWR does cause enough heat, even in the lowest loss feedline, and can spill back into your transmitter. It can cause damage to not only the cable but to your transmitter as well if it is not properly protected. That is why most modern radios employ a circuit that cuts back power and eventually ceases operating if presented with a severe mismatch at the antenna output circuit.

    Now, how does this apply to that nice, easy-to-use coax? Compared to some possible transmission lines, a good quality coaxial cable is relatively low loss. But as the type you use gets smaller, as the frequency on which you plan to use it gets higher, as the length of cable you have to use to run from your rig to the antenna gets longer, and as the type of dielectric (the stuff that separates the two conductors inside the cable) changes, the amount of signal you lose in the wire goes up, up, up. If you are feeding an antenna that is close to 50 ohms, using transmission that is near 50 ohms, and operating close to the antenna's resonant frequency, you should not have a real problem. If you have fairly good coax and, if operating on the HF bands, a run of less than 200 feet or so, you will do fine. But if the load is mismatched at the antenna, if you are seeing a higher amount of reflected power, you may be losing more precious signal than you thought. And that might explain why nobody answers your calls.

Here's what is happening. Let's say you lose 20% of your 100 watts of output power because of natural loss in the coax cable as the RF energy is making its way up to the antenna. And let's say you have a high SWR because you are attempting to operate the antenna system a long way out of resonance, or because the antenna is not designed to be used on the band you are using. Another 30% of your original RF could be getting shoved back down the cable in the form of standing waves. Well, you lose 20% of that as it goes back toward the transmitter, too, because you have the same natural loss in the cable going that way as you did going toward the antenna. You have now lost half your original power, and what's left still of the original RF energy has to go back up the feedline again! And 30% of the power that reaches the feed point gets reflected again, back down the line. As you see, the power is waning quickly!

Again, for a number of reasons, coax is an excellent choice as a feedline for most antennas, and especially dipoles and beams. It is almost the exclusive choice at VHF and UHF. But there is one very important caveat: coax is best used when feeding a resonant or close-to-resonant antenna. And there are an almost infinite number of frequencies in the amateur bands where an antenna will not be anywhere near resonant.

Well, you say, there is a simple solution! All I have to do is use the tuner inside my radio, or break out the catalog and buy an outboard tuner that will match to much broader impedance loads. That way, you reason, you can use a single dipole on a bunch of ham bands because the tuner manufacturer says it will tune up a rig to about anything.

Sorry, but that is not really the issue here. Yes, a good tuner can convince your rig that it is working into a nice, comfortable 50-ohm load, even if the antenna is ridiculously non-resonant and presents a very lopsided SWR. You can sit there and transmit all day, your transmitter running cool, not even threatening to shut down because of an excessive SWR. The meter on the tuner might say 1.2-to-1 or 1.3-to-1, so everything must be working great. Well, not necessarily. All you have really done is lie to the transmitter output circuit, fooling it into trying to send all that RF into a badly mismatched antenna. You have cranked in the correct ratio of capacitive and inductive reactance for your radio to think everything is peachy. But remember, those unavoidable standing waves are still coursing up and down your feedline, maybe invisible to your radio and tuner meter, but that reflected and re-reflected power is growing fainter and fainter with every trip up or down the coax. And only a small amount of your transmitter power is actually being sent out into space to be detected by that DX station you keep trying to call.

So coax is not a good choice at all for using an antenna on multiple ham bands? It can be! First, if you learn some antenna theory, you will discover that some antennas, such as a dipole, are resonant on some multiples of the lowest frequency band for which it was measured and cut. A closed loop is actually resonant on all multiple harmonics of the lowest frequency for which it was designed to be resonant. You can use coax and get some degree of resonance on several bands. But remember, if you cut a dipole for, say, 3.75 megahertz in the middle of the 75/80 meter band, it will really not be close to resonance in any other amateur band, except, in a stretch, 17 meters. If you play with the length, though, you might be able to move the range in somewhat and pick up some other bands, with SWR that is not such a power killer and can be tamed by most internal tuners.

Don't give up on the antenna tuner, either. While you are not solving the real problem by installing the tuner at the transmitter end of the feedline, you can, instead, put it near the antenna feed point so that you are actually tuning both transmitter and feedline to match the antenna. This eliminates a great deal of that bouncing SWR and its loss as it surges up and down the coax. Even if you put the tuner somewhere in the feedline rather than right at the feed point, you can eliminate a portion of the lossy coax, with the less cable between the antenna and the tuner, the better.

There are a few problems with this scenario. You need a tuner that is designed to be exposed to the elements if you have to put it outside, if there is not a protective structure close enough to house it. If you try to put the unit at the feed point of the antenna—the most ideal place—you need some way to support its weight. And, in most cases, you need to get voltage to the tuner to operate its components remotely. I think you can see how that complicates the matter.

So, there is no such thing as an easy coax-fed antenna that can be used on more than one ham band? Or one that is resonant for the entire length of a particular band? Not true. There are several antenna choices that can help you solve the coax problem. You can research the fan dipole, for example, in which a single run of coax can be used to feed dipoles cut for several bands. Other antennas can be designed to be relatively broad-banded. And, the truth is, SWR is probably not a big problem on a well-designed dipole with good quality coax if you only intend to use it on a single band. Even the internal tuner in most rigs will easily allow you to overcome any resulting mismatch, and if the coax has relatively low loss and the run length of your feedline is not excessive, you probably will not lose an appreciable amount of power.

But suppose you want a single multi-band antenna. A good choice is a dipole, cut to be ½ wavelength on the lowest band on which you want to use it, fed with **open wire feedline**, and tuned with a matching unit or units. There are variations of this type transmission line, such as true air-dielectric open line, so-called twin lead, window line, and ladder line. Each name describes the type design of the feedline that keeps two conductors evenly separated from each other for the length of the line. The characteristic impedance of such feedline can range from 200 to over 600 ohms depending on several factors, such as the material used to space the two conductor wires apart and how far apart the wires are.

I know what you are thinking. If a dipole is in the neighborhood of 50 ohms already, then are we not introducing a serious mismatch by feeding it with some wires that may be 600 ohms? The simple truth is, it does not matter nearly as much as it does with coax.

This type of transmission line has such low loss in a run of reasonable length that the standing waves on the line are eventually mostly radiated in the form of "good" RF, and those trips up and down the line are a relatively small factor.

There are ways to get the match closer before we depend on an antenna tuner—internal or external, at the rig end of the feedline or at the antenna feed point—to make the transmitter happy. Many hams use a current balun (a balanced/unbalanced transformer) at some point in the ladder line to step the impedance down to something closer to 50 ohms, and then running coax from the other side of the balun to the transmitter.

This also solves a rather knotty problem with open wire feed line. It is very susceptible to being effected by any nearby metal or cables. You should never run open wire feed lines down a tower leg, along a metal gutter, or adjacent to other cables or feed lines. This will almost certainly lead to problems tuning an antenna system with this type transmission line. Even trees or wet vegetation or rain or snow on the feed line can alter the performance of air-dielectric transmission lines.

There is also the problem of attaching ladder line to your radio. You most likely have coax connectors on the rear panel of the rig. Many tuners also have only coax or single wire connectors.

Once again, the answer is the balun. It may be external, outside somewhere, and coax is used for the run into the house, next to those other cables, the gutters, and the air conditioner ducts. Or it may be right next to the rig with a short coax jumper to the antenna connection on the radio in order to avoid long runs of lossy coax. Or, more commonly, next to your antenna tuner, which will be necessary to tune to the broad impedance range the antenna will present as you move about the various ham bands. The balun could also be inside the antenna tuner, a part of the circuit, if it has a "balanced" antenna connection.

A dipole fed with open wire line or one of its variations is, by definition, a "balanced" antenna. That type transmission line is called "balanced line." They go together nicely. Nature and electronics, being a part of Nature, tend to try to balance all things. However, the output circuit of your transmitter is most likely unbalanced. So is coax. So is the coax connector output of your tuner. Some tuners offer a balanced output, relying on a balun inside its case—typically a 4-to-1 type balun, changing the impedance, say, from 300 ohms at the antenna feed point to about 75 ohms on the other side of the device. But there are also special tuners designed to match the unbalanced 50-ohm transmitter output circuit to a balanced antenna system. There have been several articles in the various ham magazines about designing and constructing balanced tuners, and several manufacturers produce them as well.

Before the more convenient-to-use coax came along, amateurs, as we have seen, used open wire transmission lines, primarily because they were simple and could even be constructed using easy to locate and cheap materials. They were not as concerned as we are with the problems of matching their transmitter to antennas fed with ladder line. That was because the output circuits of transmitters in those days were much broader and adjustable. Now, with little loading to be done internally to our solid state transceivers, we have, in effect, moved the matching circuit to the radio's built-in automatic tuner or outside the radio, out onto the desktop in the form of an "antenna tuner."

However, with the desire to use an antenna on a broader range of bands, and in an effort to get as much power to the antenna and have it radiated, ladder line and its cousins are making a respectable comeback. Several distributors sell such line at reasonable cost, and their web sites even offer interesting commentary on its use, selecting baluns, and the recommendations for physically and electrically connecting it to the antenna. Other manufacturers and dealers offer spacers so you can build your own open-wire line.

So there we have it, a look at the two primary types of antenna feed lines—coax and open wire—and the various ways of using it to achieve a better antenna system. Neither is a right or wrong choice, a better or worse one. As you will discover in our hobby, there are advantages to about any way of doing something, and there are disadvantages, too. And with antennas and feed lines, the truth is that everything is a compromise, and there is no perfect system. Some are "more perfect" than others, though.

It can be a lot of fun, trying to devise ways to make those compromises as limited as you can, all in the quest for having that station on the other end of the QSO say, "You're kidding! You're not running 100 watts. You're 20 over S9 here!"

So, for the last several chapters, I have been telling you how you might be able to erect very simple antennas, and ways to put up just one and, using the proper feed line and matching device, successfully use it on multiple bands. Now I am going to backtrack and tell you some reasons why you will want to put up more than one antenna.

Let me hasten to add that my first admonition to you— new ham or old-timer—is to get up some kind of antenna and get on the air. It does not have to be perfect. You may lose many, many watts between radio and antenna. However, remember that guys often operate willingly and on purpose with very low power—QRP—and work the world on less than 5 watts. But remember, too, that they do it because it is such a challenge, not because it makes it easier.

Once you get that first antenna up and are having fun on the many amateur radio bands, it is a good time to start thinking about planting those seeds in the backyard that will eventually sprout into new and different antennas.

Chapter 11 -- What? You Only Have ONE Antenna?

First let me try to deflect potential argument with a quartet of caveats:

--If you only operate on a single amateur band and have multiple wide-spaced elements on a tower up 120 feet for that band, then this chapter is probably not for you (though I still believe you could benefit from having access to other radiators in addition to that one big beauty).

--If you operate several amateur bands and have multiple wide-spaced elements on a tower at 120 feet for each of those bands, you may already agree with my thought process here, if not the scale of its execution, but it would not hurt you, either, to have some simpler alternatives at times.

--If you live in a condo, townhome, garden home or have to answer to covenant Nazis and homeowner association zealots before you can even paint your mailbox or mow your lawn in a different direction, much less put up multiple ham radio antennas, then you probably will not be able to follow my suggestions, even if you wanted to.

--If it is all you can do to get one hank of wire in the air for whatever reason—space, money, physical ability, desire, technical knowledge, allergy to copper and aluminum—and are resolved to make do with it, then you may or may not go along with my idea here.

So here is my contention: to get the most satisfying experience from operating on the high frequency amateur radio bands, you need more than one antenna that works on the bands on which you operate—and ideally at least THREE.

Let me quickly add that I am not suggesting that you put up THIRTY antennas—three aerials for each of the ten HF bands. What I am saying is that, if possible, it is a big advantage to have a choice of antennas—and, if possible, antenna types—for each band. I am an advocate of multi-band antennas, whether you achieve it with tuner/ladder line, traps, fan-type arrangement, or black magic. With a little ingenuity and lots of poison-ivy lotion and a good supply of liniment, it is possible to have several antennas that work fine on that vast array of spectrum we have at our disposal. There are a dizzying number of sites on the Internet that give good advice on some multi-band alternatives. We have discussed several ideas already in this book. I even have some thoughts at my web site: www.n4kc.com.

Let me give you an example of how having simple options can make the difference between delirious euphoria and "Dang it!"

The other night, I was trying to work a 5L2 in Liberia on 20-meter CW. The DX cluster said he was on a certain frequency but I could not hear a thing on my big skywire loop. There was only the chaos of the pileup a few kilohertz above and a few dimwits calling him on his frequency. I quickly switched to my 130-foot ladder line-fed doublet. Yep, there he was, but just barely audible above the noise. But I had one more option—the Hustler 4BTV multi-band vertical out there in the backyard.

Click! Instantly the Liberian station was suddenly 579 (the "RST" signal report we give based on readability, signal strength, and CW tone--for AM, FM and SSB, there are only two numbers: readability and signal strength). Side benefit: on the vertical, the dimwits calling on the DX station's frequency practically disappeared because they were closer to me, and the angle or radiation of the vertical allowed their signals to skip right over me.

But there is more. An hour later, I dialed back across, just to see how the 5L2 was coming in by then. He was way, way down in the crud. Jeez, propagation was gone. Glad I got him when I could.

But then, on a whim, I flipped the antenna switch back to the doublet. 589! He was loud!

Now how could this be? Those of you who have been around the hobby for a while know that the layers of the upper atmosphere that reflect radio waves back to earth are constantly moving, shifting, and changing. It can offer a variety of heights with different angles of reflection (picture a basketball shot, bouncing off the backboard). Holes develop, too, allowing signals to zoom right past, through other layers that have interest in deflecting radio signals, allowing them to travel all the way out into deep space where amused aliens hear them, shake their heads, and make fun of us silly Earthlings.

The angles at which our emitted signals strike those obliging layers can determine whether we bag that rare one or just waste lots of kilowatt hours trying.

Different types of antennas at different heights above ground, and varying ground systems those antennas may be working against, can have a big influence on not only how much energy gets to the station you covet, but how much of his emitted RF energy finds its way to the important innards of your receiver. Both things have to happen, you see, to make a contact!

To belabor the point, here is another recent example of success through multiple antennas. We have a Sunday night group of hams who solve all the world's problems near the middle of the 75-meter band. The other night, the band was unusually long, and even ground wave signals from twenty miles or more away were lost in the static. One of our group was operating from an RV with a quickie antenna over on the South Carolina coast and most of the rest of us are in Central Alabama—about 500 miles apart. I was using the doublet, which usually does beautifully on 75, but I could copy very little of what our vacationing friend was saying.

The big loop is usually very good out to about 300 miles on 75 but mediocre any farther away (it's only 20 to 35 feet off the ground) but I decided to try it anyway. You guessed it. There our RV guy was, bragging about his view of the beach from the campground, his signal suddenly well clear of the noise on the band.

Seems to me that the ideal complement of antennas—again assuming a bunch of big, honkin' beams way up in the sky is not possible—might include one multiband wire with some height above ground, some kind of wire closer to the ground so it radiates almost straight up, and a vertical. I feel rather strongly that a vertical or some kind of vertically polarized wire (inverted L, maybe—look it up via our friends Google or Bing) should definitely be in the mix.

Bottom line is I think most newcomers would be surprised how often an antenna you do not think will work will actually do a better job than something far more elaborate. No matter your license class, your knowledge of things electronic, or how many kilo-dollars you have invested in your station, you have no control over the ionosphere and how it decides to treat your signal.

Yes, a lot of metal high in the air will work best most times. Too many laws of physics dictate that it is so. But it very often pays dividends to have more than one way to aim some RF at the sky and see what kind of lucky bounce you get.

Our hobby is on the cutting edge. I am not just making that up for propaganda purposes. We launch satellites, explore communications on a vast array of wavelengths in the radio spectrum, build software-defined radios, use computers and the Internet in some really spectacular and impressive ways, talk with astronauts on the International Space Station, do digital modes (including some we invented), TV, and more, and even contribute to technology that cures cancer and helps relieve suffering in storm-ravaged parts of the world.

Still, there is much to be said about how we use ancient technology and why. We have already talked about this as it relates to some antenna and feed line theory. Now, let us consider something that was prevalent in the earliest days of not only our hobby but communications in general.

The Morse code. You are no longer required to know it to get a license. Nor do you have to learn it and become good at copying and sending it to enjoy the hobby.

So, you ask, why should I bother learning all that dit-and-dah stuff?

Okay, I will tell you why.

Chapter 12 -- Ten Reasons You Should Learn Dah – di – dah – dit Di – dah - dah

I know. Morse code's old news. Passé. Fuhgeddaboutit! With a plethora (whatever a plethora is) of wonderful, modern digital modes, and with good, solid SSB, FM, and even a smidgen (whatever a smidgen is) of AM-with-carrier that we are able to use to communicate, why would anyone want to learn the code now that you do not have to in order to earn a ham license?

I maintain there are at least ten good reasons for everyone—new ham or OT ("old-timer")—to get out the code tapes, limber up the keying hand, build an oscillator, and learn the squeaks and squawks with which Samuel F.B. Morse and Alfred Vail blessed us way back in the 1840s.

Here are my ten. Some readers may be able to add more and I hope they will.

Reason #1: As a means of getting the message through, the code has stood the test of time. In one form or another, it has been in use for over160 years. It must have something going for it! Even now, with no requirement for even knowing a dit from a dah to become a licensed ham, there are plenty of stations to talk with if you dial down to the low end of most any amateur radio band. It is also true that contest activity on CW is stronger than ever, even breaking records for the number of logs submitted in some of them. Organizations like FISTs and SKCC dedicated to the use and preservation of Morse are enjoying booming membership. All that activity cannot be happening if the mode is dying! Or if a lot of people did not see the advantages of being fluent in those dits and dahs.

Reason #2: In marginal band conditions, CW is still far more reliable than many other modes. Some of the digital modes are as good or better, I grant you, but for a basic station, the code is still there when most everything else is unreadable. On CW, the bands open up earlier and stay open for DX longer. You can add a good half hour to either side of the gray line (the line where one part of the globe is in dusk, an especially good time for stations in those areas to work each long distances). If you study some of the modeled propagation maps, you can compare where the band will be open for, say, a 100-watt SSB signal and the same map demonstrating where a 100-watt CW signal would likely reach. The amount of additional real estate on the globe that are workable on CW is astounding. A DX station that is unreadable on SSB may be perfectly workable on CW. For me, that alone is enough reason to be proficient in using Morse.

Reason #3: In that same vein, if you are enjoying a nice QSO with someone and the band suddenly takes a dip, you can punch the rig's "CW" button and give the other OM a decent "73," ending the chat on a good note.

Reason #4: CW is legal anywhere on any amateur band on which you are licensed to operate. That even includes 60 meters, a band on which CW was once not allowed. And on 30 meters—a darn fine band for some really interesting propagation—voice transmissions are NOT permitted. It is all CW and digital modes.

Reason #5: Like to chase sporadic-E, tropospheric ducting, or other fun propagation on 10 meters or VHF/UHF? It can be a lot of fun working across the country—or the ocean!—on lowly little six meters. One way to tell if the bands are open is through beacon stations. I am not aware of any beacon stations that use any kind of voice identification or location information. They are typically transmitting in the CW portion of the various bands. That means they have to use Mr. Morse's dits and dahs to identify and give information about where they are located. How else will you know where they are or what their grid square is? Is 6 or 10 meters open to Europe or are you hearing a beacon a half mile down the road? The stuff they are transmitting sounds the same if you cannot "break the code."

Reason #6: DX! Do I need to spell it out? DXpeditions don't always use RTTY or PSK31. They almost always do CW. Because of the reasons mentioned in (2) above, and because contacts are made and completed quicker in many cases on CW than on phone, your odds of working that DX are greater. Of course, since not everybody knows or operates CW, there may be far more stations calling the DX on SSB, too, so that in itself raises your odds of nabbing the guy on CW. Sure, you can learn just enough code to recognize your call and "599," but can you be sure that station you worked was the one you saw on the DX cluster if you cannot interpret his call sign? And what if he gives QSL info, switches the split from what was spotted, or moves to another frequency or band and lets everyone know—in CW? Happens all the time. DX station on 20 meters says, "QSY 40M 7007 UP 3," yet guys keep calling him on the old frequency for half an hour after he disappears.

Reason #7: So, the only operating you do is through VHF or UHF repeaters, using FM. You don't need to know no stinkin' code! But what if you hear a distant repeater? That beepity-beep you hear on most repeaters is its ID...in CW. How can you possibly know which repeater it is or where it is located, beyond making a guess? Do you ever travel? Do you take your rig with you? How will you know which repeater you are hitting or hearing? Maybe you can find it in the directory or maybe not. In urban areas, you may be in range of several repeaters on the same pair of send/receive channels—each with a different access tone—so which tone do you use if you cannot tell which repeater it is when it identifies?

Reason #8: Simplicity. Nothing exotic about turning on and off a carrier. If you take your radio camping, on a cruise, on a business trip, it is much simpler and more effective to use CW. Add the element of QRP and you can operate about anywhere, from a bicycle to a bass boat, with basic battery power and compromise antenna. And a key, of course. Yet you will still be able to make plenty of contacts—and friends—with people who are in the same tribe you are: the CW Nation!

Reason #9: It takes less spectrum. More stations can comfortably occupy the same slice of a band when everyone is on CW rather than SSB or FM. And that is by a factor of about thirteen—150 hertz bandwidth for CW compared to more than 2000 hertz for SSB in many cases. It is easier to filter out adjacent channel interference and still maintain intelligibility, too. Many modern radios even come with a beat-cancel feature that lets you null out a particular frequency so you can eliminate that loud lout who settled in just above you and your nice QSO. That is much more difficult to do with a SSB lout.

Reason #10: It is just plain fun! I have tried many modes and I enjoy them all, but I keep coming back to the joy and simplicity of Morse. There is a certain element of knowing something not everybody else knows, too. It is like our own double-top-secret language. And you meet the nicest people there. I would have hated to have missed all the great QSOs I have had down through the years just because I decided I could not memorize and recognize twenty-six letters, ten numbers and a few pro-signs!

Now I understand that some people have greater aptitude for learning the code than others. It is more a chore than a pleasure for some. But here are a few tips that might make it less drudgery and more fun, based on my experience teaching many people the silly stuff down through the years:

Learn the code by sound, NOT by dots and dashes. "A" is "di-dah," NOT "dot dash." "B" is "dah-di-di-dit," NOT "dash dot dot dot." Learn how each character SOUNDS, not how many dashes and dots there are and in what order. That is especially true of the numbers. There is a temptation to count the numbers of dits and dahs. Your mind works much better if "6" is instantly "dah-di-di-di-dit," not a dash and four dots. See, your mind will have to go through an extra step if you learn by look (dots and dashes) rather than sound, counting the dots/dashes and then converting that to a letter. Save your brain the trouble. Learn by sound, just as you learned to talk a long time before you learned to read. Even now, when I see the code portrayed in print as dots and dashes—such as .... . ._.. ._.. _ _ _ for "hello"—it takes me far longer to figure out what they say than if I hear the characters. It is even difficult for those of us who use the code to read dah-di-dah-dit di-dah-dah, as in the title of this chapter (it spells "CW" by the way). That is the way it is supposed to be. Morse code is a sound medium, not a printed one.

Learn the easy letters first—E, T, I, M—and quickly start making words. Soon "the" (and other common words) will no longer be three Morse characters but a single sound, further saving your overworked brain from having to translate each character individually.

If possible, *have the characters you are listening to sent at higher speed* but with pauses in between. That is, have code sent at three words per minute (fifteen characters in a minute...one every four seconds or so) but the individual characters sent as if everything was at 12 or 15 words per minute. As you gain proficiency and speed up, the individual characters will still sound the same and be just as easy to pick up, except the spaces between each will be shorter.

Receive the code at a speed just a bit faster than you can comfortably copy. Just like with exercise, push yourself and you will get quicker, longer lasting results. Make yourself work to get it understood and soon you will be copying the faster stuff and asking for ever more rapid practice to be sent.

Do not get flustered if you cannot write down every single character on paper—"solid copy." Do the best you can. If you try to go back and fill in gaps or linger too long, you miss a whole bunch of other characters in the process. Then, confused, you miss still more. You will be able to get the gist of what is being said, and even be able to come back later and fill in the blanks through context.

When you are able to understand the code faster than you are able to write it down, *start taking notes and do not try to jot down every character.* You cannot write down every word of human speech in a conversation, either, unless you are a court reporter using a special machine! Those who copy fast code are doing it in their heads, not on paper. Old-time telegraph and radio operators used typewriters to copy, but it was required that they get each and every letter. You do not have to.

In your head, convert everything you see—road signs, soup can labels, letters on the TV screen—to Morse code. Try to get the word "sent" in your head (or out loud if you are alone or do not mind being thought a lunatic) before you pass the sign or before the commercial is off the TV.

Work with a friend or partner who is also learning CW. It makes it more fun, and especially if you compete to see who is the first to get to 5 WPM and, after that, to each additional benchmark.

Practice. Practice! PRACTICE! There are few things you can learn without repetition. A good golf swing? A foreign language? How to play a musical instrument? How to type? You cannot devote five minutes a week to any worthy learning activity and expect to be successful. Set aside practice time each day. There is a great boost to self-esteem when you prove to yourself that you can do something that others perceive to be difficult—or dang near impossible!

There are plenty of good sources of code to copy. W1AW sends practice every day on multiple frequencies, and when you get good, you can copy official bulletins sent via CW, too. Visit www.arrl.org or see QST for times and frequencies. Or tune to the low end of 40 or 20 meters or anywhere on 30 meters. With today's electronic keyers, most code is well sent and easy to copy. You will find speeds from tediously slow to a tinkly whir...or even some guys who sound like a cricket on crack!

I believe there are two primary reasons people do not want to learn Morse code. One is they do not see the need or have any particular interest, and especially now that the requirement for licensing is gone. I hope my reasons in this article will be some impetus for those of you in that category to give it a try. If not, that is okay, too, but you are missing some fun.

The other reason is that people simply think they will never be able to make sense out of the stuff. That they lack whatever brain cell is needed to make "di-di-dit" into "S." That is not true.

Anyone can learn the code and be proficient in its use. Anyone! It is a mindset that defeats some folks before they even try. If you are convinced you are the lone exception, that you are the only person on the planet who lacks whatever gene it takes to learn Morse code, then there is nothing I can do to change your mind.

However, if you take the attitude that "Heck, I'm not going to let this stuff beat me!" then you are well on your way to vastly increasing your enjoyment of the hobby.

I hope you will. I would love to meet you on 30 meters one night.

Chapter 13 -- The SOS Trail

"Tell me again why you brought all that radio junk along."

Vic Wheeler looked sideways at his friend and fired back the same answer he had given Chad Nelson the last five times he asked the question. And every other time he asked it whenever they hiked together.

"Okay, if you tell me why you brought that camera and tripod."

"You going to take some beautiful pictures from the summit of Mount Duran with little tin box and that fishing pole thingy with the wire wrapped around it?" Chad shot back, but with a good-natured grin.

The two hiking buddies usually spent the time on the various trails they attacked by jibing back and forth about the hobbies with which each was so enamored. Vic was a ham radio operator who loved nothing more than setting up a tiny, low-powered transceiver and vertical antenna in remote areas and seeing who he could contact around the world. Chad was an avid photographer and had a computer hard disk filled with images of beautiful scenery from most of the northwest corner of the USA.

Neither admitted to understanding the other's passion for his diversion of choice. Chad, though, was convinced ham radio was the biggest waste of time and effort ever conceived by mankind. Though Vic had been licensed when they were both teens, Chad had never quite grasped the attraction of talking to people on the radio when there were cell phones, Facebook, and chat rooms galore. And none of that technology required a license or learning that silly Morse code stuff.

The two friends had been hiking since early that Saturday morning, making one of their more ambitious journeys so far. This morning they were on the rugged trail to the top of a 10,000 foot mountain more than a hundred miles north of their hometown. They had gotten up at 5, grabbed a fast-food breakfast, and arrived at the trail head just as the sun was coming up.

The trail itself was especially tough in spots, often steep with loose gravel, but they knew the effort would be worth it, including the huffing and puffing that came with enduring that kind of altitude. The scenery was unbelievably beautiful, the vistas along the route stunning, and the feeling of accomplishment once they completed the climb would be even more satisfying than usual.

"No, no pictures with a radio, but I will make lots of guys happy with a contact with this particular summit," Vic said. That would be the most satisfying of all, Vic figured, since this would be a rare mountaintop for those hams around the world who tried to work as many of them as they could. "See, it has been years since anybody put Mount Duran on the air and we have lots of guys who chase summits when they are activated..."

"If I live to be a hundred..." Chad said when Vic paused for a breath, but then he, too, stopped talking to take in a gulp of the thin air. "...I will never understand why..."

They were still several hundred feet from the top of the peak and the trail would wind around through rock outcroppings and along a scary ledge before they eventually reached their goal. There was no shade there above the tree line, either, and the sun beaming through the thin air was already murderous.

"Hope those babies come on in," Vic said, pointing to a wall of clouds building up out to their east. "I don't know about you, but I could use the shade."

"Told you that you were getting old and soft," Chad responded, but sweat poured down his face, too. The weather at that elevation could be anything, hot and clear one minute, cold and blowing the next.

"No rain, please," Vic muttered. "Or lightning. I'd like to get the antenna up and the battery hooked up first, then I can get into the tent and still make some contacts, even if we do get some precip."

"If we get a storm, then you can sit there next to your lightning rod all you want but I'm coming back down here and hide under these rocks! It would be a shame to haul your smoking cinder of a carcass back down to Christi."

"Chad, you are a born optimist!" Christi was Vic Wheeler's fiancé and also a ham radio enthusiast, newly licensed and already working on learning the code, even if it was no longer required. She often accompanied Vic and Chad on their outdoor radio adventures, helping with the logging and even operating when Vic took his SSB QRP radio. She was busy picking out a wedding dress that weekend with her mother.

The two young men slowed their pace as they made a sharp switchback and then began climbing even harder, determined to keep ahead of any impending weather. That was when Vic looked ahead and spotted a couple of other hikers a few hundred feet above them.

The two older men had passed them a mile or more back down the trail. They had been hiking aggressively, obviously trying to make the summit before any weather rolled in.

But the pair was stopped in the middle of the trail now. One of them was bent over at the waist, obviously in some kind of distress, while the other man had him by the elbow, trying to support his buddy.

"What's going on up there?" Vic asked, pointing.

"Looks like somebody needs a blow besides you, old man."

Though the climb was quite difficult, Chad and Vic pushed harder to get to the two other men, just to see if they needed assistance. As they approached, the hiker in distress suddenly tumbled over on his face in the gravel of the trail and lay there, motionless. His partner looked up, eyes wide, a worried expression on his face, as he spied Chad and Vic coming his way.

"Help! My friend..." he said.

Chad and Vic moved managed a labored jog the last few yards.

"What's wrong with him?" Vic asked as they drew near. But he could already see the man's face was contorted with pain and he was clutching his chest.

"He thought he had indigestion...Mexican omelet on the way over this morning...but now he says his chest..."

Vic and Chad had once been Boy Scouts together and both were certified in CPR. It was part of Vic's amateur radio emergency training, too, to keep his certification current. Both men recognized immediately that the hiker was likely having a heart attack. From the looks of his face and the way he gripped his chest, it had to be a bad one.

Sure enough, the man's pulse was almost non-existent, what was there was rapid and reedy, and his lips were already beginning to turn blue. To make matters worse, the clouds that had been gathering off in the distance had quickly rolled in and it was getting darker by the second. A few cold raindrops were already pocking the dust around them and lightning flashed ominously amid the black, rolling billows.

Chad had already turned the man over onto his back and had begun to do compressions on the hiker's chest.

"You got a cell phone?" Vic asked the stricken man's partner.

The man pulled the phone from his backpack and looked at it. He punched buttons on its face then glanced up, mild panic in his eyes.

"It's dead. I forgot to put it on the charger…"

"Mine's in my vest pocket," Chad told Vic as he continued to do CPR on the sick man.

Vic pulled out Chad's phone, one of the latest and most sophisticated available and a source of great pride and derision when Chad compared its capabilities to Vic's little low-powered, Morse-code-only ham radio. Vic studied the phone's complicated screen.

There were no bars on the signal-strength read-out. They were on the wrong side of the summit or too far from the nearest cell tower to do any good.

"You keep working, Chad, and I'll run up to the top and see if I can get a signal," he reported. But just then, there was the sizzle of a nearby lightning strike and the immediate boom of thunder. Vic even felt the hair on his head rise up and felt the slight tingle of the charge just before the bolt hit somewhere above them on the mountaintop.

"You get struck by lightning, you'll never get a signal! Besides…" Chad advised, pausing to make sure he kept his rhythm steady. "Besides, I don't know if you'll get anything up there anyway. How about yours?"

But Vic was already studying the face of his own smart phone.

'Not a single bar. Too far and too much rock between me and the nearest cell tower."

Rain was falling harder now, big drops with bits of pea-sized hail mixed in. Vic quickly broke out his two-man tent and set it up over the afflicted hiker and Chad without disturbing the CPR, then tugged on the poncho he always carried in his backpack. The other hiker had already scurried beneath an overhanging rock to avoid the rain and another better-aimed stroke of lightning.

Chad walked around the area, a cell phone in each hand, frantically studying the signal strength on each readout. Neither indicator even flickered. He even tried a 911 call with each just in case but there was no success. He also ventured near the cliff to gaze back down the trail, hoping to see other hikers who might have phones that could reach out and find a welcoming cell site somewhere.

Nobody in view all the way back down the trail that he could see. The sudden rotten weather had either chased them back down or into hiding beneath an outcropping or the few small shelters lined up along the way.

"How is he?" he asked Chad, sticking his head inside the tent, rainwater dripping off his nose. The hiker's face was ashen, his eyes closed, and he was not moving except from the force of Chad's compressions on his ribcage.

"Not good. We got to get to 911 somehow and get him some help or I don't think he is going to make it."

"You think we could use a fireman's carry and get him back down?" Vic asked, but he knew, even as he asked the hopeful question, that it would be hopeless.

"Downright dangerous on that loose gravel and it will be slick as it can be after the rain," Chad answered.

"Clutching at straws, man," Vic said. "Let me know when you want me to relieve you so you can…" That was when a sudden thought hit Vic. "Hold on. I have an idea."

He ducked out from beneath the tent. He had shoved his backpack underneath the rock where the other hiker was. He ran over, unzipped it, and pulled out the little QRP (low-power) CW transceiver and its accompanying battery and Morse code key.

The antenna support was a fit-together fishing pole and a length of insulated copper wire he wrapped around the length of it.

Vic made quick work of snapping together the pole, shoved it into some soft ground in the middle of the widest part of the trail and dangled a radial wire over the side of the bluff. With a few quick hookups, he had the antenna feed line, Morse key, and the battery's power cable attached in only about a minute.

He huddled as far back beneath the rock as he could manage to keep the radio and battery out of the pounding rain, and then shoved the headset plug into the socket. When he flipped on the power switch, his ears were instantly filled with static crashes and the chirp of a few CW signals on the 20-meter ham band.

He did not cross his fingers—hard to send code that way—but he prayed for luck as he quickly pounded out, "SOS SOS SOS DE K7YOY SOS SOS SOS DE K7YOY K."

Nothing. Nothing but ear-splitting, thunder-induced bursts of static.

He sent the distress message again and again, watching the meter on his transceiver. Five watts out, and the SWR showed basically flat. He should be getting a signal out.

Please propagate, he silently begged. Please somebody, somewhere, hear me.

Then, after many attempts, a big signal suddenly overrode even the crackling electrical noise of the storm.

"K7YOY DE W3EIE K"

It was Mark in Pennsylvania, one of the guys Vic knew would be listening for him to put Mount Duran on the air that Saturday.

"CALL MOUNT DURAN PARK RESCUE HEART ATTACK NEAR SUMMIT MALE ABT 50 DOING CPR BUT BAD SHAPE," Vic sent, deliberately forcing himself to go slowly, though he knew Mark could easily copy forty words-per-minute. He just wanted to make sure he got the message. "QSL?"

"R R R R R," came the welcome reply from all the way across the continent. Mark had copied the details. Now, if he could only quickly find the contact info for the park's rescue unit. Sometimes Google could be a lifesaver, too.

The storm had moved on just as quickly as it rolled in. By the time Mark acknowledged receipt of Vic's urgent message, the rain had stopped and the first rays of sunshine broke through. A thick mist covered the trail and Vic could not even see his vertical out there in the fog.

"K7YOY DE W3EIE CHOPPER ON WAY MAKE SURE THEY CAN SEE YOU K"

"R R R R," Vic replied. "WL UPDATE TNX."

It had been two minutes since Mark answered Vic's SOS and help was already on the way.

Vic slid out from beneath the rock, ignoring the curious stares of the other hiker who had been watching him work the key and radio. Vic's tent was bright red and was set up in the trail, clearly visible from the air if there were breaks in the mist. Just to make certain, he stood nearby and waited for the sound of the approaching rescue helicopter, though he had no idea from which direction it would come.

"He still with us, Chad? I got help on the way," Vic shouted.

"I think so. Still got some color in his face and seems to be breathing. But how…?"

"Tell you later. Let me take it for a spell."

It seemed forever but could only have been twenty minutes or so before they heard the fluttering of the rescue chopper's rotor blades coming up the valley from somewhere below them. Chad and the other hiker stood and waved their arms as the pilot angled up to them, spotted them, hovered directly overhead, and dropped a paramedic and a rescue basket.

The sick hiker made it, but only after quadruple bypass surgery. Vic and Chad kept up with the man—a wealthy businessman from Seattle--following his progress and reporting it to Mark and other hams who inquired. After all, each of the ham radio operators who has assisted in saving his life had a stake in how he did.

The man's wife and grown kids were appreciative, too, and insisted on the two men allowing them to give them some kind of reward for what they had done. Vic suggested they donate a bunch of QRP kits to several local ham radio clubs in the area. They had done a good job of recruiting some young folks who were interested in going out into the field and operating. Chad suggested they locate a Boy Scout troop and give them a donation to assure the Scouts received CPR training, too.

That day, after the chopper took their patient back for medical help, Chad and Vic decided to continue their hike up the mountain. After all, they had come this far and still had most of the afternoon before they needed to start back down.

Chad got beautiful shots of a double rainbow that had been left in the storm's wake. Vic gave over four dozen ham radio stations a contact with the summit of Mount Duran. Many of them knew why K7YOY was a couple of hours late activating the location.

Mark W3EIE worked Vic again, for a "proper QSO," he said. Vic let Mark know that his efforts had likely saved a man's life, though they would not be sure for a while.

"I still don't see why you lug all that ham radio stuff up these mountains," Chad prodded, grinning, as he gazed through the lens of his camera at shafts of sun beaming through the scattering storm clouds in the distance. "How often you have to do an SOS?"

"Only takes one time," Vic responded, a big smile on his face, too. He sat back, took a big draw from his water bottle, and decided to take a break from giving signal reports on 20-meter CW to eager callers. "Tell you what. You save somebody's life with that Nikon and I'll concede the point."

"Well played, my friend. Well played." Then Chad walked over to where his friend sat on a rock, earphones on, his fingers on paddles of the Morse key, ready to get back to calling CQ. "By the way, I've been meaning to ask you something."

"Shoot."

"I am, by no means, admitting defeat. And I still reserve the right to give you grief about all that aluminum and copper you drag along with you on these hikes. But when did you say that next ham licensing class will be?"

Vic grinned broadly then mocked a faint.

Not a bad day on the mountain.

Not a bad day at all.

Even if I have managed to convince you to master Morse and jump in, the water is fine, it is inevitable that you will still want to use your God-given voice to talk with other amateurs out there on the wind. By voice, I mean several modes: AM, FM, SSB.

Technically speaking, AM actually covers SSB, too, but in this context, I am talking about good, old AM modulation with full carrier inserted, like the stations that occupy the AM broadcast band. You do remember the AM broadcast band, 540 kilohertz to 1700 kilohertz? Well, take my word for it. There is a broadcast band there in which they use AM.

There are still some hams that use this mode, too, more as a curiosity than anything else. Even old broadcast equipment is being converted to give them something to play with and allow for some very nice sounding audio.

FM certainly has its place. Most repeater activity at VHF and UHF frequencies employs frequency modulation.

But what I would like to address next is what is by far the preferred voice mode on the shortwave ham frequencies. That is SSB, or single sideband.

With today's radios, it is possible to produce a SSB signal that is remarkably efficient in its use of the spectrum and yet sounds delightful to listen to.

On the other hand, it is possible to produce SSB audio that grates, growls, and makes enemies all up and down the band. That is what we are going to discuss next.

How to win friends and influence people with your voice...on one sideband and without the benefit of a carrier.

Chapter 14 -- I See Your Lips Moving, but...

Let's open up that can of worms known as single sideband audio.

Let's don't, though, take off on a diatribe against so-called ESSB—enhanced SSB. I actually enjoy listening to those guys sometimes—you will hear them, too—even if some of them are occupying a bit more bandwidth than some prefer they do. As long as they are not plopping down on top of somebody else, where is the harm? The bands are wide enough for all of us. And I see nothing wrong with trying to get the best sounding audio one can have, even if it may not be the most efficient way to communicate.

Also, let us not jump on stations who deliberately EQ their audio—completely within legal limits but not necessarily achieving a sound you or I find pleasing—all in order to better stand out in the pack. Beauty is in the ear of the beholder. Or something like that.

The point of this chapter: adjusting our SSB audio so it is the most efficient it can be to communicate the way we want to communicate without interfering with the other guy's right to communicate the way he wants to. That is something we might designate as "The Golden Rule of On-air SSB Audio."

Like a lot of things in life, many of today's amateur radio transmitters come equipped with far more capability than some of us can handle. Or, if we have head-room on our credit cards, there are all sorts of flashy audio devices we can purchase and hook up to our radios in the eternal quest to make ours the best sounding station on the band. It is like buying a car with the capability of 150 miles per hour on the speedometer when most of us do not have the experience, reflexes, or highways to safely operate a vehicle at anything close to those speeds. That does not stop some of us from trying it if we get the urge. Now, add a rocket booster to that car or some outboard audio processing gear to that radio and let the fun begin!

Allow me to make a statement here and see if you agree. Single sideband audio should be adjusted so it is the best it can be for whatever task you are attempting to accomplish—with the stipulation that it must be legal and that it follows good operating practice, and preferably both. Note that I did not say it should necessarily sound like recording studio quality, or even that your adjusted-to-fit-the-job audio should be pleasant to the average ear.

At the same time, let me again say that many in the hobby enjoy tweaking their audio, making it sound like a broadcast station. Great! Enjoy! I love to get compliments on my SSB audio as well. I just take a lot of pride in getting it with a decent microphone that did not cost me a fortune and the EQ built into my rig of choice.

Here is the thing. If I am attempting to get the DXpedition in East Nowhere to pick my puny little signal out of the pileup, I do not need flat-from-50-to-5000-hertz response and beautiful, harmonious EQ. No, quite the contrary. What I need is a little thing called "talk power." And that, my friend, requires some careful adjustment of my modern ham radio rig.

I can crank the audio gain and compression up to "10," boost the midrange voice frequencies to the top of the pot scale, and scream into the microphone like a lunatic, but that does not necessarily give me maximum talk power. It probably gives me distortion, splatter, lots of snide comments from others in the pile-up, and—maybe most importantly if I really want to land that new country—LESS signal.

Let us talk about a couple of terms (for the newcomers because I know every seasoned ham knows what these things mean, right?).

First, why single sideband? When SSB first began to appear on the amateur bands in the late 1950s-early 1960s, the war between early adopters and the majority AM operators made the "no code" arguments look like a tea party! Oh, it was vicious! However, it did not take long for hams to see the advantages of not wasting power transmitting a big, old whining carrier or utilizing both audio sidebands, each of which carried basically the same information. Transmit the important part—the modulation information—and insert the carrier back into the mix at the receiving end. (Let me hasten to add that there is nothing wrong with using AM today. It is fun, especially if you are reviving some old boat anchor rig. I enjoy listening to AMers, too, and especially those with good sounding audio. I even jump in sometimes with my 25-watts-on-AM radio and join them.)

By suppressing the carrier and filtering out one sideband, a station needs only a fraction of the output power to reliably communicate over the same distance with the same signal strength. The reasons for this are beyond the scope of this chapter as well as my ability to explain it, but the point to grasp here is that, because of the way SSB works, there is more emphasis on how you adjust your audio if you want to fully take advantage of the mode. The peak power you put out is directly determined by *your* voice, *your* audio.

Now, how about that "Mic Gain" knob or menu setting on your shiny radio? Based on what I just said in the last paragraph, crank that gain to max and you will be loud, right? Loud equals more power, true? Not necessarily. What you will probably be doing is overdriving a stage or two in the modulation circuit. That not only makes your voice distorted and difficult to understand, but it also causes bad things to happen to the signal you are modulating. You will splatter, causing interference up and down the band. But it may be more distressing to you to realize that you are wasting precious "talk power" transmitting all that splatter and distortion in places where the DX station will never hear you. You are actually being robbed of watts that are tied up trying to transmit all that ugly, unnecessary modulation information you are casting out into the wind.

I suggest you Google "ssb modulation" or similar, or take a few minutes to read about the subject in the ARRL's *Communications Handbook*. You need every watt of signal you can get sometimes. Do not waste any of it by trying to be too loud!

There is another control there on most transceivers, one called "Compression" or "Processing." Most radios today offer you the ability to compress the audio that feeds into your radio from your microphone. This is not to be confused with data compression, in which computer files are squeezed into a smaller package. Audio compression as it is typically implemented in ham equipment, works to boost quieter sounds up, bringing them closer to the same level as louder sounds. It actually works to overcome an otherwise pretty nice thing called "dynamic range," another good term to Google.

This compression stuff has a valid purpose. It is designed to make the level of your voice more consistent, making what you are saying more understandable to the operator on the receiving end. Properly set up, the compressor takes advantage of the RF you are emitting and fills it with just the right amount of audio information. Enough to make it more readable. Not so much that you waste power on all that ugliness we just discussed.

Like the swiftness of your car or a cold beer after work, such an otherwise good thing can be abused. I remember in commercial broadcasting when the battle to be the loudest station on the band made everybody sound like gravel rattling around inside a garbage can. The modulation monitor needle did not rise and fall. It sat there at 100% and merely quivered! I worked on the air at one station with the compressor set so high that when I paused for a breath, I could hear in my headphones traffic on the street outside the studio, people talking in the lobby, and the receptionist typing on her old manual typewriter. I did not dare pause too long or the listener might have heard some most unpleasant exchanges down the hall in the manager's office since he did sometimes use colorful language.

This happens on the ham bands, too. In an effort to be loud and communicate, you actually sound abysmally grungy and muddy, and the DX station, for some reason, cannot seem to make out your call sign, no matter how clever your phonetics. Plus your nice compressor circuit is sucking up every other background sound it can, just doing its job, making every noise close to the same level as your voice.

You may have heard ham radio stations on the air with the background noise of the amplifier fan boosted until it was almost as loud as what the op was saying. Either that or he really was operating from a bi-plane crop duster. He drops his pen, it reverberates like a tree falling. Or you can hear the TV from the other side of the house well enough to tell who just got voted off the island.

Now clearly such practices as running too much audio gain or too much compression defeat the stated purpose of enhancing your ability to communicate. If you merely want to be loud, do not care how many other stations you interfere with, are not afraid of having your parenthood questioned by fellow hams, or do not mind getting mail from Official Observers (volunteers who monitor the amateur bands and advise stations of technical or operating issues) or the FCC, go right ahead and—as one of the members of the legendary rock band Spinal Tap recommended—turn it up to "11."

However, just because you can does not mean you should.

if you do want to efficiently work that DX station, pass traffic without endless repeats and fills, or have guys in your roundtable spontaneously gush about how good your audio sounds, then I have the following recommendations:

--Read the sections of the ARRL *Communications Handbook* and other source material on what is actually happening inside your radio when you speak into the side of the mic with holes in it.

--Follow the manufacturer's recommendations in the manual for your radio (You remember the manual, don't you? That little booklet you threw away with the box in your haste to get on the air with that beautiful thing with the knobs and meters? In most cases, you can download another one on the Internet. But when you do, you will still need to read it. Downloading it does not constitute knowing what it advises.).

--Use the radio's monitor function if it has one. What you hear in your headphones may not be exactly what it sounds like on the air, but it is better than nothing at all. If you can get someone to record you off the air and play it back for you or send you the audio files, that is good. There are even some Internet sites that allow you to listen to a specific frequency in near real time. One such site is http://www.3819khz.net/listen.htm. Make sure the frequency is clear before you start talking to yourself, though. Do I even need to remind you to identify, too?

--Listen to what others tell you about how your audio sounds. I know. I know. I have heard guys tell stations they sounded great when their audio really resembled nothing more than a garbage disposal full of ball bearings. Still, usually, someone will be honest with you. And do the same for others. If somebody is obviously maladjusted, tell him so (in a nice, non-offensive way) and help him hone it, if you can.

--Work with someone you trust, on the air, adjusting as you go. Everyone's voice is different. Different microphones have different specs. Some mics even allow you to choose different elements for different purposes.

--If you want to invest in outboard audio processing equipment or a better microphone, go ahead, but follow all the suggestions above. Since the first impression most folks will have of you on the air is how your audio sounds, it might be a good thing to invest a little more in being able to tailor it. But this gear is manufactured for a wide variety of potential uses and users. You can really mess up some audio if you do not watch it!

By the way, I have heard the cheap, default, throw-away hand mic that comes with the radio sound pretty darn good when properly set up. I have also heard cheap microphones intended for Skype and other computer use that sounded fantastic when the radio was properly adjusted. But I have also heard stations with thousands of dollars invested in audio processing who were barely intelligible and made my ears hurt.

--Develop different sets of parameters, depending on what you need from your transmitter's audio—one setup for DX, another for the 75-meter roundtable.

--Purge your brain of that "the higher the better" mentality. That's how Icarus staged history's first crash landing (Google "Icarus," for Pete's sake! What DID you do throughout junior high?)

So I hope we can all work for a less polluted spectrum and for more efficient communication as well as making our bands much more pleasant to tune across.

Adjustable gain and compression are nice to have under the hood, but do not run the thing into a tree!

Chapter 15 -- Why it is Easier than Ever for You to Talk to the World

Before I even get started on this subject, allow me to make clear the purpose of this chapter. It is not to minimize at all the efforts of those who successfully work large numbers of DX stations. Those who are most proficient at this aspect of the hobby of amateur radio have certain traits that I will discuss later in this piece. Since I have been observing their talent and relentlessness for a half century, you can be sure I admire them for what they do and how they do it.

Allow me to also add that this chapter may well not be for everyone. I am aware that working DX—either for awards in what some negatively decry as "5/9, 73 QSOs" or for the experience of meeting people from all corners of the world—is not everyone's cup of tea. Fine. Skip to the next chapter.

Many of us enjoy working DX, though, whether we are serious or casual about it. It is a major part of our hobby, and ties in nicely with other pursuits, such as antenna experimentation, digital mode operation, honing operating skills, QRP, radiosport competition (contests), and even stamp collecting and impressing your friends and family with your knowledge of obscure geography.

There are many amateurs, though, who are reluctant to jump in and get their feet wet. Maybe they are convinced they need light-dimming transmitted power and a ton of aluminum in the air to ever hope to enjoy such a thing. Or they see no reason to upgrade to a higher license class, assuming they would never be able to contact someone on the other side of the globe with any little peanut-whistle station they could afford to assemble once they got more HF operating privileges.

My goal here is to entice newcomers as well as those who have been around for a while to come on down and give it a go! In an attempt to do so, I am going to give five reasons why having a satisfying DX experience in our hobby is easier now than it ever has been. "Ever" being the approximately one-hundred years the hobby of ham radio has existed.

I do this from the perspective of my own recent experience. I became active once again in amateur radio in 2005 after a fifteen-year hiatus from HF. You know the story: work, kids, work, kids' sports, and work. But I got the itch, acquired a 100-watt rig, and strung up a G5RV antenna in the backyard in August of 2005. Though those were the waning days of the previous sunspot cycle, and though I still had work, more work, and work issues which left me with little time to operate, and even though I did not consciously try to lasso a ton of DX or deliberately make that the focus of my operating, I had soon picked up 75 or 80 countries.

That is when I gave myself a challenge: work 200 countries, using only 100 watts and simple antennas (along with the G5RV, I soon added a horizontal loop, a ladder-line-fed dipole, and a Hustler 4-BTV vertical to my little aerial farm). In a couple of years, and even though those helpful sunspots had become as rare as knees on a chicken, I had done it. I promise I did not work hard at it. I spent a good portion of my on-air time doing things other than chase elusive stations in faraway lands.

That, of course, is my point.

If I can do it, anybody can do it. With a modest station. With simple antennas. Even if Old Sol does not lend us a hand in the pursuit of our hobby by splashing sunspots across his face.

Here are the reasons why I think it is easier than ever for you to have a satisfying DX-chasing experience, regardless of how seriously you want to indulge or how well prepared station-wise you may be:

--Today's radios and other gear are better equipped for it. I love the boat-anchors (older radios, so called because they had heavy transformers and many tubes) as much as anyone, but when even an entry-level transceiver has some DSP (digital signal processing) and filtering, easily operates split frequencies, comes equipped with an effective noise-limiting system, does not drift even a tiny little bit, allows for some voice-processing, and includes a built-in CW memory keyer and audio processing, then anyone can be equipped to work DX. Also, when you decide to up your power, relatively inexpensive desktop amplifiers that give you 9 or 10db gain and operate just fine on regular household 110-volt power are available—including many used ones. This includes newer solid-state amps, too, though they still tend to cost a bit more than the tube-type amps do—at least from a dollar-per-watt standpoint. There are also all sorts of inexpensive digital-mode and operating gizmos that tie to your computer, giving you myriad choices for improving your capability with minimal investment.

--There are more licensed hams in more countries than ever before for you to work. I remember when it was rare to hear a Russian station. No more. There was a long period when no one could get on the air from China. Not now. Sometimes it seems there are millions of stations in Italy, Brazil, Germany and other countries. And many of those DX stations are much better equipped than in the past. They are more capable of pulling out weak signals—including yours—and they produce lots of RF for you to snag. Also, with the portability of gear and marginally less government restriction on such shenanigans, there are more and more DXpeditions operating, including many travelers who operate "holiday style" while on vacation or spending some time in exotic areas for work.

--There are more amateur radio bands on which to operate than ever. Before I drifted away from the hobby for all that work/kids/kids' sports stuff, we did not have 60, 30, 17 or 12 meters. Few thought of 160 or 80/75 as DX bands. But with all that new HF spectrum, and with advances in antennas and other equipment on the lower frequencies (see ON4UN's wonderful book *Low-Band DXing* if you want to see what I am talking about), we almost always have bands open to various parts of the world, regardless of when you can slip away to the shack for a few minutes of operating.

--Digital modes now offer wonderful opportunities to communicate with DX with very modest power and antennas. Those little squeaks and squawks get decoded sometimes even when you cannot even hear the other guy with your ears.

--And my final reason DX is easier to work than ever before: the DX clusters and other aids. Back in the dark ages, when we worked dinosaur mobile, it was no great stroke to tune 20, 15 and 10—our "DX bands"—to see what was coming in. Heck, 10 meters was dead most of the time anyway—or so we assumed, since nobody transmitted—so a quick run up and down 20 or 15 would tell us if there was anybody worth pursuing. Now, with Internet spots popping up in the window at the bottom of my logging software—that logging program is another real boon for us weekend DX fanatics—all I have to do is scroll up and down the list. It tells me instantly if anyone has spotted a country that would be a new one for me, or one I still have not confirmed. So off I go to see if I can hear him well enough to try to work him...if he is on one of the 12 bands for which I have capability and FCC authority to transmit. There are also free propagation software downloads, propagation reports all over the Internet, online forums for discussion of DX status, DXpeditions, and QSL info, and so much more that we did not have at our disposal back in the day. Back in the long-ago, we had to grab the telephone and dial up everyone on our list to alert them that Yemen was on 40. No more.

Confirming those contacts is getting easier, too. With the ARRL's Logbook of the Air computerized system, it is becoming a snap to upload contacts and get that QSO confirmed when the other guy uploads his. You no longer have to subscribe to services or wait for the monthly *QST* or independent DX bulletin to see who a station's QSL manager is or how the best way to confirm the contact might be. It is usually right there on a plethora of web sites devoted to such knowledge or on QRZ.com.

Now, let me quickly say that your success in working DX goes up greatly if you add some other things to your arsenal or have at your disposal. These include:

Power. 100 watts can get the job done. 500 watts is better. Legal limit works best. But heck, people do it all the time with 5 watts or less. I got my 200 with 100 watts or less before I went over to the "dark side" with my 500-watt tube-type amp.

Antennas. Simple dipoles and verticals work fine. (See the chapter in this book on "get on the air quickly" antennas.) Hexbeams, moxons, spiderbeams, quads or other wire beams are better. Multi-band trapped Yagis are better still. Multi-element, long-boomed monoband monsters are best under current technology. Who knows what they are working on out there in factories and garages? But remember, I got 200 with a dipole and a loop I built myself and a vertical that I picked up used for $50.

CW. If you ever plan on getting serious about making DXCC Honor Roll, or if you just like to carry on interesting QSOs with guys in other countries, you need to be proficient at Mr. Morse's code. As mentioned earlier, bands open sooner and close later for CW. DXpeditions who ignore you completely on SSB will happily log you on CW. I got about 65% of my first 200 countries on CW.

Competition-grade rig. Again, there are marvelous entry-level HF radios available at well under a grand. Guys trade up, too, so you often find them for sale used. You can work the world with them. But you can do even better with rigs that offer dual receivers, spectrum scopes, state-of-the-art filtering, and more.

There is a wide variety of radios available, and you can grow with them, depending on your interests and available disposable income. (I got my 200 on a Kenwood TS-2000...a station-in-a-box radio, with no special DX-chasing features.)

Special band segments for higher class licensees. There was a time when everybody could operate on any band. Then the FCC began setting aside some frequencies for those who took the trouble to upgrade. Technicians (and the few remaining Novice-class licensees) can work DX on HF with 10-meter SSB and CW on several bands. Upgrade to General and you get lots and lots more frequencies where you can play. Go all the way to Amateur Extra and the world—literally—is your oyster! You will have many, many frequencies where only Extras can roam free but other classes cannot, greatly thinning the herd. All the guys atop the countries-worked list are Extra-class hams. There is a reason for that. And having those exclusive segments in which to frolic makes it much easier to work DX now than it once did.

Time. That is the hard-to-come-by commodity for most of us. Fortunately, I spend a lot of time at my computer since I am an author. That means if I hear a DX station that is marginal, or if I see someone spotted that I need but I do not hear him, I just set the radio on his frequency, aim the homebrew hexbeam his way, and go back to work. Sometimes he comes up and I can log him. Sometimes I never hear him. (Sometimes he comes up and I call my head off and I do not work him, too. If it was easy, we would all have over 300 countries confirmed.)

Patience. If you get fed up after calling a couple of times in a chaotic pile-up, then you probably do not have the patience for it. Go do something else. Patience is a virtue. Some have it, some do not. Best you take up some other facet of ham radio or go find another hobby altogether rather than throw carriers on the DX station's frequency out of frustration or utter some words on the air that would be more suitable for the locker room, just because the DX station did not acknowledge you on the first couple of calls.

Operating smarts. Those come from watching, listening, and reading then emulating, trying and practicing. They come easily for some but can be acquired by most. There are books and articles on the subject. Imitate what the good ops do. Do not mimic what the dolts do, even though you will hear plenty of them. The more rare the DX station, the more likely you will hear idiots being idiots. Being rude or boorish sometimes works in getting the contact, but I suspect many of those who call out of turn, walk on other stations the DX is working, or crank their voice processors up to 11 strangely fail to make it into the DX station's log, even if the operator acts as if he put him there. Serves the bad op right!

I even hear the good DX ops chastise LIDS (our name for bad operators) sometimes right there in front of the whole pileup. I avoid throwing out a cheer when they do!

So there you go. Working DX is easier than ever. Having the thrill of communicating around the world is at your fingertips. The fingertips that twirl the knob on the front of that basic HF radio that is hooked to a decent hunk of wire strung around the backyard.

Frankly, the first 100 countries are easy. You can almost get that many in our hemisphere. I've done it with casual operation in only a few hours during a big DX contest. That is enough to get you the DXCC certificate (DX Century Club, an ARRL award). The next 100 are much more difficult. And I have a true admiration for those guys on the DXCC Honor Roll, signifying they have worked and received confirmation of the contact from just about every country there is.

But you know, I bet I get just as much satisfaction adding Azberjain or Togo, as I recently did—places I would have never have heard of had it not been for amateur radio—as those guys do in getting a new endorsement for three-forty-something on their DXCC certificate. I also truly enjoy the interesting ragchews I have had recently with fellow hams in Ireland, Australia, and Austria. That is even truer considering my modest 500-watt station and homebrew antennas.

So, if you have hesitated diving into the pileups or answering the CQ from some exotic call sign, or if you have procrastinated getting your license or upgrading from Technician because you are afraid your little signal will not reach out there to all that exciting DX, get off the dime!

There's a 9K2 in Kuwait on 17 PSK31 right now, Sweden's working CW in the General portion of 20 with a good signal, and I was just listening to several guys from Australia with 5/8 signals on 20 SSB.

I bet they would all love to have a QSO with YOU!

Chapter 16 -- The One-Hundred-Country Wager

It started the same way such things usually do: innocently and unintentionally.

Several of the members of the Spark and Spit DX Club usually got together at Junior's, a favorite local barbecue joint, for supper prior to the regular monthly meeting. It gave them the opportunity to lie, nudge, brag, cajole, praise, teach, listen and learn, and do it over a plate of inside-sliced smoked pork and greasy onion rings, all washed down with glasses of cold, sweet iced tea.

W4OOU, Clark Lawson, who, everyone knew, had over 300 DX entities worked and confirmed (because he regularly told everyone it was the case) was decrying the recent lack of sunspots and the deplorable condition of the amateur radio bands when it came to reaching out to other parts of the planet. He even threw in a jibe or two against the increasing numbers of new operators on the air who, he felt, were "gettin' in my way and ruinin' the hobby."

"It is a darn struggle," he proclaimed between bites of his sandwich. "I feel sorry for you newbies, trying to work anything new and exciting with these conditions lately. I have not heard Oceania or Southeast Asia in months. Even Africa is weak as water nowadays. Tough, tough, tough. And all of these new no-code licensees would rather call and talk than listen, butcherin' up the band something awful. They make it a real challenge for us veterans who know how to do it right."

Grace Wade was KB4JJO, a relatively recent licensee. She usually attended the pre-meeting dinners with a pencil and notepad, eager to make notes and learn more about the side of ham radio that had attracted her the most so far—working DX. She rarely said much, other than to ask questions or for clarification.

Each of the supper club members looked her way when she suddenly leaned forward and responded to Clark's diatribe.

"Clark, I agree it's been a little tough propagation lately, but I think there are still plenty of DX stations we can work. Just the other night…"

Clark waved his sandwich in her direction and shook his head.

"Listen, missy, I've been at this ham radio DX thing since before you were making mud pies and getting your first training bra. I'm saying this is the worst sunspot cycle we've had in a hundred-fifty years and it is almost impossible to work DX these days…especially for them that came up the last few years and don't know which end of the coax is which," he proclaimed.

Grace pursed her lips, narrowed her eyes, and was clearly on the verge of letting Clark have it with both barrels. Then she thought better of it and spoke much more calmly than she had almost done.

"Don't think I totally agree, there, Clark," she told him, smiling slightly. "The solar flux is way on up there and if those solar storms will just die down for a bit, I think there is great propagation on all the bands."

Clark snorted and took a big swig of his tea.

"Solar flux! I don't give a rip about no solar flux! I know what I hear coming out of my speakers. A new ham today would be lucky to work a dozen countries the rest of the year, propagation being all gone to heck and all like it is. And even then, he better have a big-gun station, power, and a beam way up on a stick. There is no DX to work. None. Zip. Zilch."

Grace shook her head and looked across the table at him sideways. There was an odd look in her eye, the others around the table would later report. A decidedly determined look on her face.

"I still disagree," she told him, clearly resolute in making her point. "I believe a decent station with an operator who knew what he was doing could work plenty of DX, even if this cycle is kind of slow getting going."

The other hams gathered for supper were surprised at how solidly Grace was defending her contention, and especially against an experienced, imposing DXer like W4OOU. And, admittedly, a blowhard like W4OOU, who was never bashful about picking a position and sticking to it, regardless the logic against it.

Clark Lawson set his tea glass down hard and pointed an index finger at Grace as he lectured her.

"I appreciate you sticking to your guns, little lady, but I'm right on this one. You can't work no serious DX on the bands today, way they are. End of argument."

The rest of the bunch never knew if it was the "little lady" or simply the fact that she was convinced she was right, but what happened next became part of Spit and Spark DX Club lore, a story that would be shared among the group's members for years to come.

"How about a little wager, then, Mr. Lawson?" Grace asked with a sly smile and a hint of a sparkle in her eye.

"What you got in mind?" Clark responded immediately. He had a slightly quizzical look on his face but he clearly welcomed a challenge. Especially when he knew he was correct. W4OOU was accustomed to having his strong opinions challenged, but always by the more experienced hams, the ones not afraid of his bluster—and his considerable knowledge and experience. Not some young newcomer, a General-class licensee, and a woman, to boot. Now he was wary, wondering if he was being set up.

"I have something in mind," she told him, even as she contemplated how best to prove her point and put Clark in his place once and for all. Truth was, she had no idea what the challenge should be.

Lawson smirked, looked around at the surprised faces of the other hams, and slapped the table. He was in his element. He was ready for a rumble, even if he had little respect for his opponent.

"Well, come on with it. If it makes sense, I'll bite." He crossed his arms and settled back in his chair, ready.

Grace Wade sat back in her own chair, took another sip of her iced tea, put her napkin on her empty plate, and looked across the table at Clark Lawson. The smug look on his face only made her more determined now. She could not back down. And besides, she was as convinced she was right as he was.

"I can work one hundred countries in one hundred days, starting tomorrow."

Lawson's eyes went wide and his jaw dropped. Then he burst into laughter. The others gathered around the table were also shocked. Most were pulling for Grace to come up with a worthy challenge to Clark. Now, she may have just come up with a bet on which she had no chance of collecting.

Work one hundred countries in one hundred days? With the current conditions, a relatively inexperienced ham radio operator—one with a fulltime job, kids, a husband, and an average station—had very little chance.

"Hon, let me get this straight," he said, his voice more condescending than derisive. "I believe you have a decent radio out there at your place but it's only a hundred watts, right? No amplifier. And some kind of gizmo wire beam. Ain't enough with the bands like they are these days. But the big thing you don't have is experience. You been licensed how long? Year and a half? You might just want to reconsider making this wager…little lady…before you bite off more brisket than you can chew up and swallow."

The "hon" and the second "little lady," delivered more as a slur than a term of friendliness, sealed it. Even if Grace had doubts about whether or not she could win the challenge she had impulsively cast out there amid the empty plates and barbecue crumbs, she decided she had no choice but to go through with it now.

"No, I think I can win it," she said, trying to sound confident. "I know I can win it." She glanced at the wall, at a chalkboard on the other side of the table where they sat on which Junior listed his restaurant's specialities. "I'll wager a full rack of Junior's baby-back ribs with all the fixings. And a gallon of sweet iced tea. You on, Clark?"

Even if W4OOU had any doubts, he could not back down now. Not in front of all the others who now looked his way to see if he would accept the wager. But there were no doubts in his mind. None whatsoever.

"Well, darlin', there is no way. Bands are terrible. You, being a newly licensed, no-code General class ham with a pip-squeak station, would have a hard time working one hundred countries in one hundred days anyhow, but not now. Not with propagation conditions like they are." He looked around the table at the assembled hams, saw the looks on their faces that pretty much agreed with his assessment, and then leaned back in his chair. "I'll go you double-or-nothing. You lose, I get a rack of ribs with the fixings. You win, you get two racks of ribs. And I'll even throw in my Vibroplex Blue Racer bug key."

The intake of breath around the table was audible. Everyone knew how much Clark loved that old Morse code key, a true collector's item. W4OOU had just raised the stakes far beyond some dead pig and sweet iced tea. That only confirmed just how much Lawson wanted to prove his conviction.

Grace Wade did not even flinch. She reached across the table and shook hands with Clark, ignoring the barbecue sauce on his fingers.

"You're on!"

On the way out of Junior's, one of the other hams walked alongside Grace, talking quietly.

"Grace, I appreciate you standing up to old Clark, but you don't have to do that. He's mostly harmless and he's forgotten more about propagation and working DX than most of us will ever know. He may just be right on this one."

"I know all that, Tom, but I think I'm the one who is right," she told him. "I keep up with the solar weather, I spend lots of time studying the reverse beacon network and watching the DX clusters. I think we are about to have a good run for the next few months. And I just can't stand old Clark's attitude toward folks who are new to the hobby. Somebody needs to put him in his place and I think I am the very one who can do it."

"Hope you are right," Tom said, shaking his head. "But that old so-and-so will be hard to live with if you don't win."

She smiled at him.

"Way to put more pressure on a gal," she told him, but she realized that her grin was likely not nearly as confident as she had hoped it would be.

The first week was great. Conditions on 20, 17, 15, 12 and 10 were moderate to very good and KB4JJO quickly logged thirty countries, mostly in Europe, South America, and the Caribbean. She and Clark had agreed they would work on the honor system, that confirmations would not be necessary, but she still hoped to get as many QSL cards and Logbook of the World (the ARRL computer logging site) confirmations as she could, just so there would be no backpedaling or cries of foul.

By the end of the first fourteen days, Grace had logged another dozen different DXCC entities and felt even better about her chances. She was actually thinking about getting 150, just to press the point. Almost halfway to her hundred with almost three months to go!

Piece of cake. Or, rack of ribs, in this case.

Then, on the way to drop off her girls at daycare and on to work one morning, Grace half heard something on the car radio. She reached and cranked up the volume so she could hear the newscaster over the girls singing in the back seat.

"...and scientists say the coronal mass ejection occurred on the side of the sun facing earth, so the resulting solar windstorm would likely disrupt radio communications on our planet for most of the week upcoming. Of course, it will also create beautiful displays of aurora borealis—the northern lights—as far south as the central part of the USA."

"Oh, crud!" Grace said, out loud.

"What, Mommy?" her oldest daughter responded.

"Nothing, darling. Nothing." No way to explain solar flux and A and K indexes to a four-year-old. Grace admittedly only had a basic understanding of all that stuff herself. But she knew it

236

would mean the shortwaves would be mostly hiss and buzz with few workable signals for a depressing chunk of the remaining time she had to get to her one-hundred-countries-worked.

Sure enough, that night 20 meters was a mess. Only a few 8s and 9s chatting, barely discernible at the noise level, complaining about the terrible band conditions. 40 was mostly static, too. And she did not have an antenna for 80 or 160, the only other bands that might offer up a stray country or two in the midst of all that junk from an active sun that had been whirled her way.

She tried not to think about Clark Lawson pointing his finger at her, lecturing her, but his image kept popping into her head as she turned the dial and listened to the dead shortwave bands.

A week later, things had picked up just a bit, but now sunspots were suddenly few and far between and the ham bands remained less than spectacular for trans-continental communications. Grace stayed up late one night and picked up both Australia and New Zealand on 20-meter CW and then yawned and half dozed at her desk the next day. Her boss just shook his head and rolled his eyes when she told him she had been on her ham radio chasing countries most of the night.

"Most people watch TV," he told her. "Not you. You do whatever it is you do with that radio stuff!"

"Work DX."

"Whatever 'DX' is. Work, I know about. And you have plenty of it to do, if you can stay awake."

But he was good-natured about it. He had even talked about joining her at a club meeting, maybe getting his own ham license someday, after hearing how much fun Grace was having in the hobby.

One of the big DX contests was coming up in two weeks and that was Grace's ace in the hole. With any luck—and just the slightest bit of help from the gods of propagation—she figured she could nail most of the rest of the countries she needed during that frantic forty-eight hours. It was the single sideband portion of the event and she knew a female voice was worth a lot when it came to getting the attention of the DX stations. They tended to stand out from the pack of males shouting and screaming for the distant station's ear.

"How you comin' along, sister?" Clark asked her at the next pre-meeting barbecue supper.

"I'm on schedule," she told him, preferring to play it coy. Not the time to brag, for certain, since she actually was well below where she had hoped to be by that point.

"I sure got me a craving for some ribs," Clark prodded. "Should I be getting my fork and spoon ready, sis?"

"Not just yet...brother," Grace told him, and the rest of the hams at the table laughed at her gig. "I'll make it. No problem."

She only wished she was as confident as she made every effort to sound like she was.

The DX contest helped but not nearly as much as she had hoped. Grace kept hearing the same countries over and over—Italy, Germany, Japan, the big contest stations on the same islands in the Caribbean—and she just moved on, dialing up and down the bands, looking for new call signs, new countries, hoping for shifts in propagation to other parts of the world where plump DX fruit hung, ready for the picking.

By the last minutes of the contest on Sunday evening, she was dog-tired, thankful that her husband, Greg, had taken the girls out for a movie and hamburgers and did the dishes and laundry, all so she could concentrate on her quest. However, she was thoroughly disappointed that she had only added a couple of dozen more countries to the total.

Not time to panic yet, but for the first time, doubt was starting to overtake and lap Grace Wade's confidence.

Slowly, maddeningly slowly, she picked off a few more countries over the next few weeks, watching the tally build ever so slightly each time she ran the report in her logging software. With two weeks to go, she finally nailed Iceland, number ninety.

Fourteen days left and still ten short. No matter how much she twisted that VFO dial and studied the DX clusters scrolling down her computer screen and chased prefixes up and down the spectrum, it was becoming more and more obvious that she was in trouble.

She still gave no hint of her progress to W4OOU and the rest of the gang at Junior's Barbecue.

"I'm in good shape," she told them.

"Sure you are, little gal," Clark responded with a belly laugh. "I'm listening to the same mess as you are. About the only openings we get are during the daytime and you're working. And all the 'appliance operators' come out on the weekend and scream and holler and muddy the water for the rest of us. This solar cycle is a bust and I'm convinced you picked the wrong time to try to prove a point."

Maybe so, she thought. But until the next Sunday night at midnight local time, she was not yet dead. On life support, maybe, but not yet dead.

Though she was tempted to take some vacation days and really go out with a bang, Grace decided to not do it. She had promised Greg and the kids that they would take a week and go to the beach over Thanksgiving and she only had three vacation days left. Family over hobby. Even if it meant listening to Clark Lawson gloat for the next year.

Then she hit a couple of good nights on 30 and 20 meters. Central Europe gave her four new ones. A DXpedition on some island she had never heard of near Antarctica was another one. On the third night, South Africa, Madagascar, and several countries in the Middle East were rolling in on 20 SSB. She was patient, relied on every trick she had so far learned, and bagged all of them before the band went bottoms-up about one in the morning.

Over coffee on the last Saturday morning of her one-hundred days, Grace ran the report one more time in her logging system.

"99 countries worked. 84 confirmed."

For the first time since the first few weeks, Grace was confident she would win the wager. Only one more country needed. One stinking country. And she had most of the weekend to find it and get it safely in the log. Maybe even add a couple more for good measure and drive home her contention that it could be done.

As soon as she got a load of laundry going and the breakfast dishes done that morning, she went into the shack and fired up the radio. There were some strong signals but the static crashes were atrocious, near deafening.

Grace brought up her web browser and checked the weather radar. Wow! A solid line of storms was approaching her location. She quickly disconnected her antennas and shut down the radio. No time to tempt fate. No chance to get that last country if lightning frazzled her station.

It was late afternoon before the rough weather had moved on and she felt it safe to get things hooked back up. Now, even through the nearly continual bursts of static, she could tell the bands were, for the most part, dead as a hammer.

She tried them all. Even six meters. Maybe a stray sporadic-E cloud might bring her the Bahamas or one of the few Caribbean islands she had so far missed. There had been no stipulation on the bands she could use, either. Anything in the ham radio spectrum.

But there was nothing. Hiss and a local beacon station. That was it.

Grace almost hated to check the solar weather report on her favorite DX site. Sure enough, it showed conditions to be "Poor" on every one of her most likely bands. Another CME, another burst of solar wind, had erased the ham bands at the worst possible time for her and her quest. At least if she had any hope of winning her wager with Clark Lawson.

Why, she asked herself, had the gods of RF propagation allowed her to get to 99 countries in her pursuit and then left her stuck there? So close and yet so far away.

Still, she had Sunday. Church came first. No problem. The bands still sounded lousy and there was not a single DX spot for a country she still needed, but surely she could pull one more out of the murk. Just one more.

She wondered during the service if it was wrong to pray for good propagation. She was sure other hams had so she went ahead and did it, too.

Greg treated them all to pancakes at IHOP after church, but Grace's mind was obviously on getting back to the shack and conjuring up one more new prefix.

"Your mind's on the ionosphere, isn't it?" Greg asked her as he poured more syrup on one of the girls' pancakes.

"I'm sorry, honey," Grace told him, smiling. "I guess this thing got a little out of hand and there's nobody to blame but me."

"Hey, you gave it your best shot. You may even have lit a spark for me to go ahead and get my ham license. Anything that means as much to you as this has must mean it is worth doing."

"Have I mentioned lately that I love you, Mr. Wade?"

"No, mostly you've just mentioned ZLs and GMs and PY5s." He grinned as he said it and she blew him a kiss across the table.

By six that evening, Grace was ready to admit defeat. The bands held nothing new at all. There were now some very big signals from various parts of the world but they were all in areas she had mined already. Well over 300 different "countries" were on the ARRL list—countries as far as ham radio went, at least—and she had managed contacts with only 99 of them in her given one-hundred days. But now, in the waning hours of the wager, not a single new one popped up anywhere on the bands.

Grace almost passed up the usual two-meter FM ARES training net (Amateur Radio Emergency Service) on the local repeater at 8 PM. She figured she could use the final few hours to scan the bands some more, praying for a morsel. Still nothing, though, so she flipped on the two-meter radio and listened to the various stations check in from around the area, then joined in when it was her turn.

To add insult to injury, just after Grace checked in and was acknowledged by net control, W4OOU chimed in as well.

"This is W4OOU…Whiskey Four Oscar Oscar Uniform…with no traffic but listening to a bunch of dead HF bands tonight." And he laughed as he said, "Over."

Grace knew that was for her benefit.

Now she was clutching at straws. Maybe she had incorrectly logged somebody. Sometimes one number or letter could make a difference in the country where that ham operated. She called up the logging program and scrolled through the last three months' worth of contacts. Everything looked to be in order.

As she listened to the other check-ins on the net, she re-ran the report of countries she had worked one last time. 99 of them. Not 100. 99. The pixels on the screen did not lie.

On a whim—and maybe to remind her not to be so quick to jump into a fight again with somebody who knew how to throw a punch—she printed out a list of the countries she had worked. Sometimes looking at a hard copy as opposed to the computer monitor made mistakes pop out. There was also the chance that she might find an easy one she had missed and jump back on the most likely band and call "CQ Mexico" or something. She printed out a list of the countries she still needed to work, just to compare.

But Mexico was on the "worked" list. So was Canada. Cuba. Puerto Rico. Alaska.

The two-meter net was just winding up and she was not sure she had the heart to even turn the AF gain back up on the HF radio. She had lost. That was clear. Close would not be nearly enough to silence a guy like Clark Lawson.

Then, as she studied the list on the print-out of unworked countries, her mouth suddenly fell open. She almost dropped the cup of coffee from which she was about to take a sip.

No way! No baby-back-rib way!

The net control had just re-set the repeater controller to normal use and closed the net. Before anybody else had the opportunity to grab the channel, Grace picked up the FM radio's microphone.

"W4OOU, this is KB4JJO. You still there, Clark?"

The courtesy beep had hardly sounded before Clark responded.

"KB4JJO, here's W4OOU. I figured you would be trying to get those last dozen or two DX countries you need instead of jawin' here on the repeater with me, seeing as how time's up in a few hours. Over."

"Clark, let's go down to five-two-simplex for a minute. Okay?"

There was a pause then and Grace could just imagine the smirk on Clark's face.

"Well, sure, but if you are about to throw in the towel, we can just do it here on the 88-machine for everybody to hear."

Grace was well aware that not only the Spit and Spark DX Club, but the whole membership of the regular ham club and just about everybody else in that part of the state were aware of Grace's challenge and had been trying to get an update for the past month. Grace had decided to not let anyone know where she stood. It would have been tough enough if she had missed by a mile. Getting to within one would be an especially hard bit of news to report.

"Everybody will hear how it came out soon enough. Let's go to five-two so somebody else can use the repeater. KB4JJO, going to simplex."

"Happy to oblige, little lady. W4OOU, QSY."

Clark only lived a few miles away so the conversation on the simplex frequency would be no problem. Grace could only imagine how many others who had been listening to the exchange on the 88 repeater had dialed down to the simplex frequency to try to hear what was going on.

W4OOU transmitted first.

"KB4JJO, this is W4OOU. You figured out how to move that little radio knob down to five-two?"

Oh, Clark was in rare form this evening. Confidence had that effect on such people.

"And a good evening to you, too, Clark," she told him. "I was wondering, after the storm yesterday, how my two-meter beam is doing. What's my signal report?"

Again, a moment of silence. She figured Clark would be wary now, afraid she was going to tell him she had made the goal and had a hundred countries in the log. She grinned as he came back to her and waited for the requested signal report.

"And I figured you wanted to give up, maybe admit you were wrong about how good the bands were. But I'll play along 'til tomorrow night. You will be at the barbecue supper, won't you? I'd like to go ahead and collect my ribs then if that is okay with you?"

Grace held the microphone tightly, trying to keep her voice from trembling.

"We can take that up tomorrow night, Clark. What's my signal report, though?"

"Well, little missy, you are 5-by-9. 5-by-9 right here in the United States of America. And the handle is 'Clark.' And I like my ribs with dry rub and a big bowl of sauce on the side."

He laughed uproariously before he un-keyed his microphone.

"I appreciate it, Clark. You are 5-9 as well. See you tomorrow night, and 73."

Clark was still laughing, wheezing, as he came back one more time.

"I have to admit, you are one tough cookie, girl. You won't admit defeat on the air but you're willing to face the music in front of the Spit and Spark guys. See you there. Have a good evening...if you can find another couple of dozen more countries you need to make the hundred! 73!"

Grace slumped back in her chair as his signal dropped away.

The usual gang had gathered at Junior's the next evening. It was clear that Grace was not going to admit she had lost the bet until after they had all finished their meal, even though Clark continued to goad her and try to get her to give them some kind of hint of how close she had come.

Most figured she had come close. Not a person at the table felt that Grace had accomplished her goal.

"Look, girlfriend, no shame in putting up a good fight," Clark poked at her. "I say if you got more than sixty or seventy countries, that's something to be proud of. No shame there, lady."

Then several of the others conceded they had side bets going on the DX challenge, some backing Grace, others figuring she could not possibly pull it off. Clearly they were anxious to hear the outcome, too.

Finally, supper was done.

Grace Wade retrieved her purse from beneath her chair and pulled out the print-out from her logging program. She slowly unfolded it, dramatically smoothed it out on the tabletop, and handed it across to Clark Lawson.

The grin was frozen on his face as he took it. For the first time in over three months, there was a hint of doubt in his eyes.

Would she have given him a print-out if she had not gotten her hundred?

Had this rookie, this no-code General-class newcomer, this inexperienced DXer with 100 watts and a wire beam actually done it?

Grace's face was noncommittal, as blank as most of 20 meters had been the past week. The other hams glanced from her to Clark and back, looking for some clue to the outcome.

"Well, I'll be a monkey's uncle," Clark finally said, quietly, weakly, as he noted an even one-hundred log entries on the print-out. "This little gal has done gone and…"

Then, as he looked at the last page of the logbook print-out, Clark's eyes grew wide and his mouth flew open.

There, on the last line from the logbook, the one numbered "100," was the entry:

"0221Z, W4OOU, 146 mhz FM, 59 sent, 59 received, USA."

Somehow, in the heat of trying to get all those countries worked, Grace had not worked a single station in the United States. There, in the last hours before falling one entity short of the goal, she had picked up the final country contact she needed to make her 100.

And that wager-winning, last-minute contact had been provided by none other than W4OOU.

Chapter 17 -- Everybody's S-Meter is Correct!

What is the first bit of information we typically glean or give when we begin an on-air conversation with another amateur radio station? The signal report, of course.

Later, we talk about the weather, brag about our stations, decry the lousy lack of sunspots, but first, we want to know what kind of signal we are getting to the other guy's radio. We want to make sure we give the other op an accurate idea of how well we are receiving his or her transmission as well.

It's a courtesy, of course, but it also helps us get an idea of how the band is behaving so we can gauge if we can continue the chat and determine what other parts of the world are there on our doorstep for the taking. It can certainly help each operator involved in knowing how well his station is performing. And in some cases, it gives us a chance to inform the other ham of a problem with audio, keying, or other aspects of the signal he is putting out there on the air.

Fortunately, there are a couple of standardized ways of letting a station know how well his signal is making the haul from his place to yours—the "RST" system and that dancing little back-lit indicator there on the front of your whiz-bang new radio: the ubiquitous S-meter.

"RST" originated way back in the early days of telegraphy as a way to quickly and concisely inform a station how well he was being heard. It is a 3-digit number with the numbers standing in order for "readability," "signal strength," and "tone." Readability is a five-number scale while the other two parameters are nine digits. The scale, according to publications from the American Radio Relay League, is:

Readability:

1 - Unreadable

2 - Barely readable, occasional words distinguishable

3 - Readable with considerable difficulty

4 - Readable with practically no difficulty

5 - Perfectly readable

Signal strength:

1 - Faint signals, barely perceptible

2 - Very weak signals

3 - Weak signals

4 - Fair signals

5 - Fairly good signals

6 - Good signals

7 - Moderately strong signals

8 - Strong signals

9 - Extremely strong signals

Tone (CW only):

1 - Sixty-cycle AC or less, very rough and broad

2 - Very rough AC, harsh and broad

3 - Rough AC tone, rectified but not filtered

4 - Rough note, some trace of filtering

5 - Filtered rectified AC but strongly ripple-modulated

6 - Filtered tone, definite trace of ripple modulation

7 - Near pure tone, trace of ripple modulation

8 - Near perfect tone, slight trace of modulation

9 - Perfect tone, no trace of ripple or modulation of any kind

Operators can also add a "C" if there is a chirp on the keying or a "K" to denote the presence of key clicks. There's also a quaint "X" indicator that can be included if the station's signal demonstrates the frequency stability of being "crystal-controlled." And of course, the "Tone" number is not used for voice communications, though I think I could make a strong argument for making some kind of audio evaluation a third number for voice reports. Truth is, though, on voice you can simply inform the op that his audio sounds as if he is gargling a duck. That is easier than scrambling to find a number to attach to the issue and then have him scramble to see that that number means he sounds as if he is gargling a duck.

The obvious problem with this method—even a system that has stood the test of time for almost a hundred years—is that it is totally subjective. What exactly is the difference between a signal that is "barely readable" and one that is "readable with considerable difficulty?" And how do you bring yourself to give a guy a "4"—readable with practically no difficulty—when it's so close to being a "5"—perfectly readable?

Oh, and how many of you could describe what a "rough AC tone, rectified but not filtered" actually sounds like and would know such a thing if you heard it?

One thing that prompted me to include this chapter was hearing a station the other day give another ham a signal report of "Five by two!" I suppose it is possible to be perfectly readable with a very weak signal, given a quiet band, but hardly likely, and especially considering the conditions that particular day. He was probably more like a "four-two" or even a "three-two" since the generous signal-report-giver was clearly having trouble hearing the other station.

I also received a QSL once that has a CW signal report of "3-8-9." Hmmmm. Maybe it was my fist (the way I send Morse code) that made me difficult to read despite my strong signal with a perfect tone!

Of course, I am almost always "5-9-9" or "5-9" to DX stations in pileups, even if they have to ask me to repeat my call a dozen times or insist on calling me "K4NC," so I'm obligated to give them the same report right back, right? You know, of course, that DX stations working thirty stations a minute or stations operating in the heat of a contest do not really want an accurate signal report, nor are they likely to give you one. It is 5-9-9, all the way. You just gunk up the works horribly if you insist on doing him a 3-5-8!

And I hesitate to even bring up those QSOs in which one station's audio is so distorted or hum-ridden that he can hardly be understood and the fellow on the other end of the circuit doesn't even mention it to him. I've even heard such accolades as, "Good audio!" when the offending station was using so much compression I could hear pots and pans rattling in the kitchen and he sounded as if he was talking through a pillow. He certainly should have been smothered by *somebody*! But is it his fault that he has atrocious audio if nobody tells him he sounds like loud, distorted mush? How can he fix it if some nice, overly diplomatic reporter tells him instead that he sounds perfectly fine?

So, thank goodness, we have another way to give honest signal reports, one that is totally accurate, unbiased, the same no matter what the make of the rig or the disposition of the operator. I speak of the S-meter. It is the omnipresent little device available on most every commercially made piece of ham gear or SWL receiver, and since it is—by definition—a meter, it has to be correct. And since all the operator has to do is say where its needle points when giving a signal evaluation, it removes all prejudice from the resulting report.

You realize, of course, that everything said in the previous paragraph is delivered with sarcasm and a firm tongue in cheek.

Another thing that prompted this chapter was a discussion on the Yahoo Kenwood TS-2000 reflector—a subject that crops up on a semi-regular basis. Inevitably, someone will do an A/B check of different radios, using the same antenna, listening to the same station at about the same point in time. The result in the latest round of give-and-take was that the TS-2000's S-meter seemed to read considerably less than the other radio's did. Was it possible that the Kenwood's receiver was that much worse?

Maybe. But inevitably the station being sampled was just as readable on both radios. In some cases, the S-meter read nothing at all on the 2K and S-3 or S-4 on the other rig, yet again the station was equally readable on both.

Dang quirky radios! How is that possible?

Let us take a quick look at what an S-meter is without being overly technical. In actuality, most S-meters measure the voltage across the radio's automatic gain control (AGC) circuit, though that is hardly universal. Few are—dare I say it?—

accurately calibrated. Likewise, few are linear across their entire scale either. They are actually designed to give the user a RELATIVE measure of signal strengths arriving at the receiver. More on the meaning of RELATIVE momentarily, but I am not talking about your spouse's kinfolk.

The "S" in "S-meter" stands for "signal strength." Thank goodness! I am still miffed that "E" means "voltage" and "I" is "current" when you abbreviate those basic units of electronics. The markings on the scale of the meter—the "S" units—are based on our old friend, the "RST" system above.

Things were pretty wild and wooly in the old days of the S-meter, but back in the early 1980s, the International Amateur Radio Union agreed to recommend that an S-9 reading on an S-meter, indicating "extremely strong signals," would be defined as -73 dBm, or a level of 50 micro-volts at the antenna input to the receiver if the impedance presented there is 50 ohms. That's for HF frequencies. The recommended standard is different for VHF, but let's leave that alone for this article. Just understand that a bunch of responsible folks got together and standardized what the S-meter calibration *should* be. Remember that: *should* be!

Furthermore, the IARU suggested that each S-unit gradient represented a difference of 6 dB. That is a power ratio of four, or power doubled and then doubled again.

So, since the IARU came up with a recommendation for a standard, the S-meter police must guarantee that all S-meters everywhere work exactly the same way and are completely accurate devices, right? You know the answer to that!

Still without getting technical—and primarily because I do not understand it all either—suffice it to say that the manner in which most S-meters work makes them anything but accurate, rarely linear so that each unit on the meter equals a 6 dB difference, and almost completely inconsistent from one radio to another, including radios made by the same manufacturer.

Also, the accuracy of a signal report, including an S-meter reading, is still dependent on the operator and his setup. Is my signal really 40 over S-9 when I hear that wonderful report, or does the guy just need a QSL card from my state for Worked All States?

Is that an average of the peaks or a momentary peak on that rapidly dancing little meter? If I am not even moving his meter, could it be that the op over yonder runs with his pre-amp off, the way I usually do on 160 through 40, or is my signal really lucky to even be reaching his radio? And we have not even gotten into other parameters that affect my signal strength at his place. Minor little things like antennas and propagation!

What the S-meter can do just fine is give a RELATIVE indication of strength between two or more incoming signals. Relative meaning compared to another signal.

"Don, you are peaking about S-9, but your buddy down the street...running the same power and about the same audio setup...is about 20-over S-9. You may want to do some antenna work!"

Your meter may be inaccurate and nowhere near the IARU's hopeful standard and dismally without linearity, but it is inaccurate and non-standard and non-linear for everybody. Just do not try to compare the S-meter reading on your Goshdarn 3000 Plus with your buddy's Heckfire Pro IV. They will not be the same...necessarily.

So here is the good news. Everybody's S-meter is completely accurate! Accurate as long as he is using it to give RELATIVE signal strength reports.

Permit me a brief illustrative fable.

When I was a youngster, I was helping my dad (SK WA4AZJ) with a carpentry job. He asked me to cut him a 2X4. I asked him how long it needed to be. He answered, "About as long as a piece of rope."

I stood there perplexed, saw in hand, for a bit, trying to figure out where to start cutting, until he finally let me off the hook and gave me the exact measurement for the board he needed. Lots of things in life are relative.

Maybe I can apply that same bit of whimsy next time I begin a QSO.

"What is my signal there, old man?"

"Oh, you're peaking about two inches with peaks to the screw-head on the old S-meter. You even got up to the `n' in `Kenwood' a couple of times. Good signal! Now about that QSL card of yours that I need…"

Chapter 18 -- A Dark and Stormy Night

A deep-throated rumble of distant thunder rattled the two cans of soda pop that rested on the metal patio table. The two people sitting there on the dark, screened-in porch hardly noticed as they chatted with each other. The rain had let up noticeably and now they could hear the droplets tinkling metallically as they hit the bottom of the nearby downspout. The tree frogs sang happy songs of damp contentment from the far end of the backyard and a cool breeze felt especially refreshing in the wake of the late-afternoon heat that had them sweltering prior to the thunderstorm.

"Sorry, Jack," one of them said to the other as he reached for his drink. "I could fire up the generator and we could get to work but I suspect the power will be back on shortly anyway. Probably just a transformer tried to gargle some rainwater."

"Aw, don't worry about it, Mr. Nielsen," the other person said, his voice much younger, obviously still in the process of changing from kid's to man's. "If we don't get it fixed tonight, we still have a few days before my ham license shows up in the database and I'm legal."

"You may as well start calling me 'Tom.' That's what we hams do, you know, regardless our relative ages. First names and call signs. That's the way we know each other." Tom Nielsen took a sip of the fizzy drink. "I think we can get that radio fixed up pretty quickly anyway. They had a problem with the PLL losing synch on some bands as it aged and got knocked around and it's usually just a matter of tweaking."

Jack Marshall took a big swig of his own soda.

"Hope so. You don't know how many lawns I mowed to be able to buy that radio. I wish I knew as much about radios and antennas and electronics as you do, Mr. Nielsen...uh...Tom. I've got so much to learn and I don't know where to start."

"That's the great thing about this hobby. Amateur radio allows you to follow your own interests and, if you want to, keep right on learning stuff for the rest of your life. Or not. Nobody says you have to." Lightning flickered on the distant horizon, a bit dimmer now. "Heck, I learn something every day, still, after almost thirty years in ham radio and engineering. The hobby's still evolving and you can change with it. Or not. Nothing says you have to. You can go at your own pace, and don't let anybody tell you different."

"Maybe so, but I wouldn't know where to start working on that old Kenwood. I just appreciate you looking at it for me at the swap meet. I've sure enjoyed listening in on the bands that work. Even with the dipole, I heard stations in Germany and Sweden and even the Canary Islands. I had to break out Dad's atlas to find where the Canary Islands were exactly."

"See, learning geography, too! Without even realizing you were getting educated. This hobby will make you smarter no matter how hard you resist."

Jack was quiet for a bit, and then he said, "I appreciate you taking so much time with me. You know there are a few folks around who aren't quite so welcoming to newbies."

Tom cleared his throat.

"I suspect that's true in any hobby or pursuit. Some think it's a fraternity and you have to haze people who want to join it. Others are just protective. They don't want anything to change or evolve, even though change and evolution are inevitable. Some are just plain ornery and anti-social. But the hobby's big enough for all of us, whatever our interests. Shoot, the way I look at it, the more the merrier. You guys bring a new perspective on things, fresh blood. That helps keep us old-timers young."

The door behind them opened with a squeak of its spring and someone stuck her head out from the darkness inside of the house.

"You two guys out here growing moss?"

"Hey, hon," Tom said. "You want to join us out here? It's probably getting warm in there with no electricity. There's a breeze."

"Don't mind if I do," she replied, shining a flashlight their way. "What's the topic? Football? No. Let me guess. Ham radio!"

Tom took his foot and slid one of the empty patio chairs her way.

"Wrong! Women. I've been warning young Jack here about the weird and wily ways of the female of the species."

"Just because you've been married to one for twenty-two years doesn't make you an expert on the subject, mister," she responded with a laugh.

"Mrs. Nielsen, I was wondering..." Jack started, but she interrupted him.

"You may as well start calling me 'Heather.' That's how you'll do it once you get on the air."

"Okay...Heather. Mr. Nielsen...uh, Tom...and I just went over that. It's going to take some getting used to, I guess." He took another draw on his pop. "How did you get started in ham radio? There don't seem to be as many women in the hobby as men."

Heather Nielsen stretched out in the chair, enjoying the rain-cooled breeze.

"True, but I think that's changing. We're more comfortable with computers and computers are more and more a part of amateur radio. I think that makes more gals comfortable with the technical side. We're more social than guys in some ways, too, and get a kick out of meeting new people and talking to friends on the air. It'll take a while but there is definitely a positive trend. Same thing with you young folks. How old are you now, Jack? Fifteen? I think a lot of bright kids are getting tired of Facebook and Twitter and are looking for something that is a little more of a challenge, more diversity and more things you can do than just post stuff on a wall. And so they can learn stuff that'll help them decide on and get ready for a career, too. Yeah, I know. You can call somebody in India or Australia on your smart-phone. But I dare you to dial a number at random and find somebody on the other side of the world with whom you have instant rapport—something in common with—like you do with ham radio. And use a radio station you put together and an antenna you built to do it."

Jack thought for a moment and said, "You know what? You sound like a commercial for ham radio! I'd guess from your call sign that you've been a ham a long time. Right? What got you interested in the first place?"

"I tell people I inherited the hobby," Heather said with a chuckle. "My dad and mom were both active hams. My brother got his license, too, but he never took much interest in it. I resisted it as long as I could. Back then, the last thing you wanted to be labeled as was a 'nerd.' Especially a girl nerd. Kiss of death in high school social circles. Who wants to date a gal who knows Morse code and understands Ohm's Law?" Heather paused for a moment. The thunder was even more distant and the lightning flashes no more than flickers on the far horizon. "Then there was the hurricane."

"Hurricane?"

"Yeah. I grew up on the Mississippi coast. We had a category four when I was about your age. Just to please my dad, I had passed my Technician exam but had not been on the air more than a few times. I worked hard not to let word get out at school, you know. 'Heather the ham.' One of the football players I had a crush on nicknamed me 'Betty Beepity- beep' when he found out. Then the storm hit. All the phone lines were down. Cellular wasn't as widespread then but there was practically no phone coverage of any kind. TV and radio were mostly off the air. Even the local police and fire departments lost their communication towers. My family and several other local hams were on the air day and night for better than a week. I spent most of the time at the hospital emergency room, talking with hams set up at the police station and fire department, letting the medical personnel know who was on the way and what their injuries were. I also initiated plenty of health-and-welfare traffic, letting family members know their folks were alive and at the hospital. I was even interviewed by one of the TV network reporters and that was my first taste of broadcast journalism."

"Wow!"

Heather tucked her feet beneath her and took a deep breath.

"Wow, indeed. I know we saved some lives that week. And avoided a lot of worry on the part of family members. For the first time, I realized this radio junk was more than just a geeky hobby or glorified CB radio. The rest of it slowly grew on me. I'm still not that technical, but I enjoy some contesting and DXing, especially on PSK31 and CW. But my favorite thing is a net I'm a part of every morning on twenty meters. We've got a great bunch of people, most of whom I've never met in person, yet they're like my BFFs."

"'Hen party' is what I call it," Tom interjected. Heather cuffed him on the arm. "Ouch! Watch it. That's my soldering hand. I may need that to get Jack's Kenwood going if the power ever comes back on."

"So you were both licensed before you got married?" Jack asked. "Was that how you two met? I didn't see that as a benefit in any of the ARRL propaganda I read. Finding your soul mate through amateur radio."

Tom and Heather both laughed.

"I was that stereotypical geek," Tom said. "For as long as I can remember, I loved taking things apart and figuring out how they worked. I read an article in a magazine about amateur radio and I was hooked. There was a guy several blocks away that had a tower and beam in his backyard and, even though I was a bashful lad—I know it's hard to believe—I walked right up and rang his doorbell. Thank goodness, he didn't shoo me away like the pest I was. His wife made cookies while we went to his shack for a tour. He worked—I don't remember for sure—but I think it was DX. Of course, the next county would have been DX to me. Throwing out a radio signal that could tickle somebody's antenna halfway around the world was nothing short of magic to me. Next thing I knew, I was going to club meetings, studying, building power supplies and a little one-tube transmitter and about the ugliest antennas you've ever seen, and then I had my ticket. There were years I was less active than others, what with girls and cars and high school and then going away to college, but little did I know where this hobby would eventually lead me and how it would disrupt my life."

Heather laughed again.

"That's where I come into the story."

"Yep, that's where this wench rode into my otherwise wonderful life. I was at the university, freshman year, taking that English course that even would-be electronic engineers have to take. I had already noticed the pretty girl who usually sat to my right in that class but since I was still that same shy and retiring type, I didn't have the gumption to say anything to her. Then, one day I noticed she had an earphone in her ear while the teacher was up there droning on and on about some dead poet or another. She's listening to the Eagles or the Doors, I thought. Those were rock groups back in the Dark Ages, see. Anyway, I couldn't decide if that was cool or if she was just a ditzy blonde."

Heather cuffed him again.

"You never told me you thought I was ditzy!"

He ignored her and went on.

"But then I could see that it was a handie-talkie poking out of her purse. This ditzy blonde—sorry, cute gal—was scanning the two-meter repeaters instead of listening to Professor Calabash."

Heather laughed.

"See, I really knew how to impress the guys, didn't I? I never dreamed that old HT would land me a husband! Truth is the local ARES net was a ton more interesting than Dr. Calabash."

"After class, I went up to her and asked her which repeater she was listening to. Don't ever tell me I didn't have a gift of gab!"

"Last of the great romantics! I have to admit, that was the most original pickup line this gal has ever heard. 'What repeater you listening to, little lady?' That's okay, I got a free hamburger at the cafeteria out of the deal. And the rest, as they say, is history."

Jack listened to the tree frog serenade for a moment.

"So you guys got married and have lived happily ever after on the ham bands?"

"Not hardly," Tom said. "We were both way too busy with school...both of us had to work our way through...to do much with radio. I had a little QRP rig in the dorm room and a piece of wire out the window, but I mostly just listened while I studied. And got on the air some when I went home between semesters until my mom moved all my gear into the closet to make room for a bunk bed for my little brothers."

"I only had that HT at school," Heather said. "And still do, in a drawer around here somewhere, but it doesn't even have a tone board in it and I'd probably play heck trying to find a battery that would fit it anymore. I tutored football players for tuition so that kept me busy, anyway. I did steal Tom's QRP rig a few times and set up under a tree on the quad. Guess I had long since gotten over being labeled a nerd. I remember I worked Japan once with 5 watts and that piece-of-wire antenna. And got some strange looks from the guys playing flag football out there when I started squealing and doing a little jig over working the JA."

Tom chuckled as he gazed into the darkness and continued the story.

"We had a ham club on campus but in that day and time it was mostly inactive. The club station was in the Student Union but it looked like something out of the early days of wireless. We kept saying we were going to fix it up and get it back on the air but never quite got around to it. Calculus was kicking my hind end."

"But we made it, didn't we, Tommy?" She squeezed his arm. "Our wedding was the day after graduation. Tom had an offer from an engineering outfit here in Atlanta and I landed a job with a little newspaper out in Douglasville. Later I hooked up with one of the radio stations here in town, doing news. The program director was a ham, and even though he was inactive at the time, I know that connection helped me get my foot in the door."

"You're sounding like a ham radio commercial again, darlin'."

"Sorry. There have been times when neither of us touched a mic button or CW key for months. Sometimes we didn't even have a working station on the air. But the hobby has always meant a great deal to us. And not just because it brought us together in the first place or helped us get our careers going. Seemed like every time the bug bit again, we enjoyed radio even more than before. Always something new to experience. New people to talk to. New technology to take a look at. I love it!"

"Couldn't tell, could you?" Tom asked with a wink, but young Jack couldn't see it in the darkness.

"You guys have kids?"

"A daughter," Heather answered.

"She's up at the university, majoring in spending mom's and dad's money," Tom added.

"She a ham, too?"

"Naw," Tom replied. "We exposed her to it but didn't push. She never developed an interest. Again, like most hobbies, ham radio is not for everybody. Some never get the itch. You can't force it. You nurture it, help those who show an interest. Answer their questions. If the spark is there, suddenly the light will come on one day."

As if on cue, the lights inside the Nielsen house flickered and then remained on. The air conditioning unit just beyond the end of the covered porch roared to life and the ceiling fan over their heads spun on.

"Thank goodness!" Heather said. "Just in time for *Desperate Housewives*." Tom rolled his eyes. "Hey, mister, we all have our guilty pleasures. I see you watching those pawn shop shows."

She stood and stretched.

"I really appreciate you guys telling me your story," Jack said. "And for the sodas and cookies."

"You are welcome," they both replied, in unison.

"Let's go get that old Kenwood working," Tom said. "If it is easy as I think it is, we might be able to chase a little DX with it on 20 meters before the band goes to sleep for the night."

"You boys have fun," Heather told them as she headed for the door. "I've got supper dishes to clean up now that we have light. But if you hear anything exotic, let me know so I can log 'em, too. The DVR will catch my show."

"So that's your game. We find 'em, you work 'em."

Jack Marshall picked up his soda can and followed his new friends into the house, toward the basement room where Tom's and Heather's radio shack was located.

Six weeks before, he did not even know these folks, other than having seen Heather doing news reports on the local CBS television station. Now they treated him like an old friend or a favorite nephew. But most of the club members—except for a few curmudgeons who seemed to resent anyone who did not get a license in the 1950s or who dared to enter the hobby before his sixtieth birthday—had shown the same welcoming ways. There were even a few guys and gals his age in the club.

"You really think we can get the rig going on 20 meters?" he asked Tom.

"Maybe. And I've been thinking about a simple wire vertical antenna you could hang up in that big pine tree in your backyard. Might be just the ticket for 40 meters..."

Jack grinned. Grinned and wondered why he had waited so long to get started in this amateur radio stuff.

Chapter 19 -- You might be a "REAL HAM" if...

Those of you just getting started in the hobby probably check out the various web forums dealing with amateur radio. If so, you have almost certainly seen those occasional arguments when someone makes a post in which he or she attempts to make the point that someone is not a "REAL HAM" unless he or she meets certain arbitrary criteria.

Those arbitrary criteria typically include such requirements as passing a code test to get licensed, using equipment with tubes in it, or being able to build a transceiver from scratch, using only a pie tin and a handful of grab-bag parts from a swap meet. Never mind that those licensed today have no option of demonstrating their Morse code abilities, and with today's slick commercially available radios, building something is not required and constructing one's own gear is just another aspect of the hobby that one can pursue if desired. Or not.

Still, I have decided that I need to come up with my own list of benchmarks that might establish whether or not a person qualifies. With apologizes to a certain comedian who has made a gazillion dollars with his "You might be a redneck if..." shtick, here goes my feeble attempt at noting what it might take to be considered a "REAL HAM:"

--If you have a ham band antenna on all four fenders of your car, the roof, in the trunk lip, and another one attached to the trailer hitch and held in place with an alligator clip and duct tape...you might be a "REAL HAM!"

--If your wife...sorry, "XYL"...asks you to help bring in the groceries while you are chasing a rare one and you yell back, "QRX! QRX!"...you might be a "REAL HAM!"

--If you can recite the numbers of every driver, modulator, and final amplifier tube in every Heathkit, Drake or Collins transmitter or amplifier ever made, and name the best idling grid current for 90% of them...you might be a "REAL HAM!"

--If when you were a teenager, you tore open the cases of your little brother's "Flash Gordon" walkie-talkies just to see if you could modify them to work on 10 meters or used the pans from your sister's Easy-Bake oven to breadboard a code-practice oscillator...you might be a "REAL HAM!"

--If you have ever tried to bring up the local repeater while riding in a funeral procession...you might be a "REAL HAM!"

--If your kids...sorry, "harmonics"...know your call sign, your grid square, and your 10-10 number, but not your middle name...you might be a "REAL HAM!"

--If you have at least a half-dozen different sets of hilarious (at least to you and the guys on your 75-meter roundtable) phonetics for your call letters...you might be a "REAL HAM!"

--If you have more countries confirmed than you have dollars in your 401-K and more bucks invested in your tower, rotor and tri-band beam antenna than you have in your retirement annuity...you might be a "REAL HAM!"

--If you have ever taken an HT to church or a scanner to the courthouse while on jury duty...you might be a "REAL HAM!"

--If you painted the walls of the new playroom downstairs in the colors of the resistor color code...you might be a "REAL HAM!"

--If you ever chopped up your wife's...sorry, XYL's...patio furniture to build a Yagi for 15 meters...you might be a "REAL HAM!"

--If you have ever attempted to use a gutter downspout, the hubcap from a '93 Buick, your dog's food dish, your neighbor's rose trellis, the vent hose from a clothes dryer, a wicket from your mom's croquet set, or a one-quart metal Thermos bottle (with or without coffee) as an antenna...you might be a "REAL HAM!"

--If your read the ARRL *Repeater Directory* or the latest catalog from one of the big "candy stores" while taking your daily "constitutional" ...you might be a "REAL HAM!"

--If you know the formulae for Ohm's Law and Kirchoff's Law and can read a Smith Chart from 100 feet but have no idea who Paris Hilton is...you might be a "REAL HAM!"

--If you typically go to hamfests wearing your "Hams do it with frequency" tee-shirt, a "KNOW CODE" belt buckle, at least two HTs clipped to your belt and an earpiece for each in your ears, a pith helmet with a 440 ground plane sticking out the top, and a blinking-LED button with your call sign on it...you might be a "REAL HAM!"

--If you know the prefixes for every DXCC entity as well as their beam headings but you do not know your oldest kid's...sorry, "first harmonic's"...birthday...you might be a "REAL HAM!"

--If you ever flagged down a local utility bucket truck and tried to bribe the guy to hang some ropes and pulleys in the trees in the backyard...you might be a "REAL HAM!"

--If you call beers "807s," money "green stamps," your house your "home QTH," your car your "moe-byle," your base station your "shack," the FCC "the Friendly Candy Company," anything a salesman tells you "Bravo Sierra," the big brouhaha at the last club meeting "a Charlie Foxtrot," your wife your "XYL," and your kids "harmonics" ...you might be a "REAL HAM!"

--If you ever tried to convince your fiancé that Dayton, Ohio, has replaced Niagara Falls as the Honeymoon Capitol of the World and that the first part of May is absolutely the best time for a wedding...you might be a "REAL HAM!"

--Of course, if you MET your fiancé in the flea market at Dayton when she tried to jaw you down on the price of a Hallicrafters HT-37 with a bad power transformer...you might be a "REAL HAM!"

Hey, we may get silly about our hobby some times, but it is sure a heck of a lot of fun!

Chapter 20 -- What Have You Done for Me Lately?

As you can imagine, when I became active again in amateur radio in 2005 after a twelve-year hiatus—kids, job, writing, all competing for time and attention—there were numerous things that had changed in the hobby while I had been away. I have just observed my 50th year of being licensed and I can honestly say that I am as enthusiastic about ham radio as ever. I am glad it was still around—and better than ever—when I returned to it. And I am deeply thankful to those who roll up their sleeves and make it even better. Or who work hard to keep it in existence.

Many of the changes I noticed when I came back to the airwaves are good ones: new bands, new modes, satellites, computer/radio interfaces, transceivers in tuna cans, software-defined radios, continued growth within our ranks, new countries opened up to the hobby around the world, and so much more.

Other changes? Well, maybe not so good in retrospect. In many cases, though, one man's wonderful evolution is another man's travesty. But is that not the case in all aspects of society?

One thing I noticed has unfortunately not changed at all. Way back in 1961, when I was an awe-struck 13-year-old on a tiny farm, fascinated by all this radio stuff and how it allowed me to go way beyond our few acres, there was one thing I picked up on right away. When I twisted the dial on my Hallicrafters receiver, I would invariably hear some people who vociferously condemned the American Radio Relay League. It was, according to them, the League's fault that single sideband and its incessant "duck quacking" was becoming the ruination of amateur radio. The League's fault that kids (like me) could get a Novice license without knowing how to build a linear amp from old TV parts and only needed to copy code at five words-per-minute to join "their" hobby. Those old guys in Connecticut's fault that transistors were replacing tubes and *QST* was running ads for factory-made gear and the bands were full of contesters two weekends in November. Heck, even the low point in the sunspot cycle was somehow the fault of the American Radio Relay League.

I suppose I should not have been surprised that I still catch those same kinds of charges today, though it is not a Hallicrafters anymore on which I hear them. And it extends to media that would have been science fiction to me back then. There are new ways of doing it thanks to the Internet, online forums, and blogs. Believe me, the freedom to express one's opinion—anonymously—is rarely wasted.

It comes to mind now because of not only some snatches of conversation I have heard on the air but also because of discussions I sample on the various ham radio discussion forums, including the new one on the League's own web site.

"I won't use Logbook of the World because I hate the ARRL and all they stand for."

"*QST* is no good anymore and once upon a time, that was the only reason to join the League in the first place."

"The ARRL has sold out to the big manufacturers—the contesters—the EMCOMM guys—the moonbouncers (take your pick!)."

I suppose it's human nature to complain, and nowadays it's easier than ever to squawk—often anonymously or virtually so. No one has to back his charges with evidence or even validate his opinions with logic. The League is a big, attractive target, too. They, by their very nature, serve a large constituency with varied strong opinions and a multitude of axes to grind. There is no way they can please everyone, nor should they try. After all, if you try to be everything to everybody you end up being nothing to anyone.

However, to get the dialogue going, I am going to pull out some typical complaints similar to those I have seen and ask some pointed questions about each of them

"The ARRL has done absolutely nothing for me or the hobby! They are just there to oscillate their egos and make money."

OK, will you or some other organization be there representing amateur radio interests at the next ITU World Radiocommunication spectrum conference? If so, have you done your homework and have data to support keeping what frequencies we have already and the backup to try to secure some more? What the procedures are and what it takes to participate? Heck, do you even know what, where and when it is?

Can you get an audience with the White House disaster preparedness staff, as the ARRL recently did? Or negotiate a letter of understanding with the American Red Cross? And what have you done to defeat recent legislation in the U.S. House of Representatives (HR 607) that would take our 70 CM band and auction it off for wi-fi use? Were you even aware of that bill? Do you or some other ham radio organization have a lobbying voice and legal help in Washington, DC? Do you have attorneys standing by to help hams with interference, antenna zoning, RFI complaints, and other issues?

Frankly, if I disagreed with 95% of what the League did and stood for (which I do not!), I would still be a happy, dues-paying member just for the things mentioned in the previous two paragraphs. We absolutely must have a solid, strong national organization representing a significant number of amateurs in order to do these sorts of things. Do you have that clout? Do you know of anyone else that does?

Why haven't you produced videos and brochures to promote the hobby? When was the last time you submitted a press release to the media or provided a clearinghouse for news about the hobby? I must have missed all that literature you and your other organization produced to invite others into the hobby. Your license manuals. Your study guides and various levels of technical publications that you have written and published and sell for just enough to make back the cost of production.

Do you and that shadowy other organization of yours have the ability and reach to nurture and support clubs? Or the wherewithal to administer the Volunteer Examiner program? Have you built up a spectrum defense fund to fight those who would displace us? Where is your bulletin station? Your code practice transmissions? Your technical assistance department? How do I subscribe to your weekly propagation report, your contest newsletter, your DX update, your version of QEX? What contests do you sponsor?

I guess I must have missed your informational web site, like the one the ARRL maintains (still needs work but it's sure better than yours!). And why have you hot built and de-bugged or paid somebody to do a competitor to Logbook of the World if you don't appreciate the League's efforts in that regard?

"OK, but those equipment reviews in *QST* are bogus. They have been paid off by the advertisers to only give positive reviews."

Could you point to a single instance in which the ARRL Lab review of a piece of gear was intentionally wrong or misleading? I can show you examples in which shortcomings of tested equipment were noted and discussed. Those were for gear from major manufacturers who also happened to be regular advertisers in *QST*. If you were a member of ARRL, you could go online and read every single review published and see for yourself.

By the way, there is nothing to keep you from purchasing equipment, taking it into your well-equipped lab, using your vast knowledge of electronics as you test it to your heart's content, trying it out, and publishing your evaluation for the world to see. I know we all would trust your evaluations and findings completely because you have no biases whatsoever.

"These were the same yo-yos who came up with 'incentive licensing,' which almost killed the hobby!"

Wow, you guys have a long memory! I cannot even remember just how much the League had to do with the final actions by the FCC in that regard, but I will bet they were following the guidance of the majority of their members at the time and were convinced that the changes would be in the best interests of the hobby. Were you a member then? Did you tell your director or Section Manager how you felt? Did you submit comments in response to all the Commission's notices?

Or did you just squawk to your buddies on 75 meters?

Here's the thing. The League is a membership organization and it operates as a representative democracy. Members elect directors who set the policy. Members are able and encouraged to meet and communicate with their directors. I see mine at every hamfest I attend. He must have few weekends to be with his family or be on the air, so I hope he gets a huge salary for his service.

Wait. He doesn't get paid? Oh.

I receive regular email updates from him and other League officials, nationally all the way down to section level. His contact information is on the League's web site and inside *QST* every month. My director represents what he feels is the will of the members in his division and what is in their and the hobby's best interest.

Do I always agree? Naw. But I know the majority rules. And I can vote my guy out next time if he consistently ignores the benefit of my wisdom.

Shoot, if I think I can do better, I can run for the job myself and then I can straighten this bunch out. If you really do not like the way the League is representing you and amateur radio, run for office!

"QST is a rag! Take away the ads and the minutes of that last directors' gabfest and there is nothing left. Where are the technical articles? How come the DX section isn't bigger? Where are the UHF articles? It's too technical for most of us with all those articles by electrical engineering types! The articles are dumbed down so much my Pekingese could build most of the projects!"

I heard these exact complaints fifty years ago, yet even then I was thrilled each month when *QST* showed up in the mailbox. Of course every column or article is not necessarily of interest to me, but my interests change. I had never done PSK31 until a few years ago, nor had I ever slowed down to read a sentence of any article about the mode. Now, I not only gobble up all I can find in the magazine on the subject, but I can go back online and read all those articles I passed over for all those years. As mentioned before, those in our hobby have a broad range of interests and it is impossible to slant the magazine so all articles only appeal to you and your niche.

Have you made suggestions to the editor? Given feedback to the League about the articles, pro or con? Even better, have you written and submitted any articles on your subject of choice? Has your Pekingese?

Remember, too, that *QST* is the official journal of the League. It is required to use the magazine's pages to communicate what your elected and employed officials have been doing. You would be complaining about all the secrecy if they didn't! Skip it if you don't want to read it!

I know a little bit about advertising and publishing. If it were not for the ads, you would pay a hundred bucks an issue for

QST. Well, maybe you would not because you are a cheapskate, but that would probably have to be the cover price. Be thankful that those manufacturers continue to buy ad space so you can afford to get the pub as inexpensively as you can.

Besides, many of us enjoy the ads. We dream and drool and keep up to date on who is doing what new stuff. If we suddenly need some part or gizmo, we can likely see it advertised in *QST*. And even cooler, the magazine and the League have strict policies in regard to claims that can be made in those ads.

Look, if you think you can publish a better magazine, have at it. Nobody's stopping you. You can even do it via the Internet without buying paper and ink. Hire a staff. Sell ads. Pay writers. Knock yourself out.

Oh, and good luck with that. If you can do it so much better than the League, you should be able to knock them off in no time.

Same with other League publications. I hear folks complain that they are too expensive, too big, too small, not updated often enough, updated too often. Get off that web forum where you do all your moaning and complaining and write a book yourself. Take photos. Draw schematics. Test your projects. Find a publisher. Get distribution. Fill that gap you feel the League is leaving. Make a fortune!

And then there is my favorite:

"The League is a grand conspiracy. They are trying to simplify the license test so much to get more people into ham radio so they can make more money. That is all these crooks want—to sell memberships, books, repeater directories, certificates—so that is why they have dumbed down the exams so much."

If you have not heard this line, you have not been listening, Hallicrafters or not. Ah, the conspiracy theorists!

Maybe in your state of denial you have never read the section on the ARRL web site about the organization's primary purpose. It is, and I quote: "To promote and advance the art, science and enjoyment of Amateur Radio."

It makes sense to me that this would include doing many things to encourage growth in our hobby. How else do we bring in new blood that will develop even more new modes, equipment designs, and operators to assist in emergencies? You have ideas on how to do that? Catch your Section Manager or Division Director at the next hamfest or drop a note to him or her. Do not keep all those brilliant ideas to yourself, expecting the League to intuit.

Oh, and you can file a request for rulemaking with the FCC any time you want to. Get them to toughen up the exam so only the best and brightest—like you, of course—have a snowball's chance of getting into your exclusive fraternity. Make them require that anyone getting a license knows it all first. That way they will not have to keep learning afterward.

What? You haven't tried to change the rules yet? You would rather blame it on the ARRL every night on 20 meters than actually trying to get things changed to suit you?

Frankly, I don't know what the salaries are of the guys who work at ARRL HQ. But I would bet they are comparable to or even less than what people in similar positions of responsibility and running an organization of this complexity make. I do know that if the paid staff is not doing their jobs, the division directors—and, by proxy, me, N4KC—have the ability to redirect their career paths.

Hey, I know the ARRL really does not need me to race to its defense. And I know the criticism is relatively isolated. It is just that it is so loud and screechy and persistent, like a heterodyne on top of that DX station I am trying to nab.

292

I will bet you that guys spit and spewed at old Hiram Maxim way back in 1914, too, when he was just getting this ham radio national organization cranked up.

Also, if I have been hearing all this kibitzing and second-guessing for fifty years, it probably is not going away tomorrow either.

However, I do hope this little epistle will make some of you stop and think the next time you utter some of those quotes I have highlighted here. Stop pontificating, join your organization, and make positive suggestions so you can be a part of changing the way things are done if you do not like them. Make the League better if you believe you know how.

Or go start your own organization and make yourself Head Poobah.

"I'm just one guy. I can't change the League. Why bother?"

If that is your attitude, then let me suggest that you shut your yap. If you are not willing to be a part of changing something to reflect your opinion of how it should be, then kindly shaddup.

Or maybe you do not really believe in democracy.

Chapter 21 -- The Saddest Words I Know

"I don't know how."

My precious granddaughter was at the kitchen table, working with her new microscope, trying to see some brine shrimp eggs. No matter how hard she tried, or how many exasperated noises she made, the viewer remained dark.

"You have to adjust the mirror so the light reflects through the slide," I told her.

"But Grandpop, I don't know how!"

"Did you look at the instructions? Did you try to move the mirror around and figure it out?"

"No. Fix it for me."

Ah, I was being presented with a perfectly grand teaching moment.

It would have been much easier to simply adjust the microscope so she could see the tiny eggs and hurry back to my easy chair and copy of *CQ Magazine*. However, I decided to give her a quick tour of her new toy, lecture a little bit about optics and reflections, show her the section in the instruction sheet that addressed the subject, and sit her down to read it. Then I made sure she tried what she read until she got the results she sought.

Of course, she took one quick look at the infant shrimp, shrugged her shoulders, and ran off to something more flashy and glittery. But that is not the point.

The saddest words I can imagine are when someone says, "I don't know how," and then stands there, waiting for someone to do it for them.

Look, I know that not all of us are naturally and incessantly curious. Sometimes we have no desire to know how something is done or how it works. We just want it done or working. There is nothing wrong with that.

I have no interest in learning how to replace the brakes on my car. I am perfectly willing to pay somebody to do that. While the mechanic changes them out, I get to do something I want to do or that makes me money to pay for the work. Meanwhile, he does his job, feeds his family, and the chances that the vehicle will actually stop when I want it to stop are ratcheted up considerably.

New kitchen cabinets? I am convinced I could study and experiment and buy a fortune's worth of tools and waste a bunch of expensive materials and learn how to build some perfectly good kitchen cabinets. Still, I choose to hire someone who already knows how, who already owns the tools, and who does a good job of installing them correctly the first time.

Though I do not acquire a desirable skill when I let someone else do it, I also realize that it is a bit of knowledge I would likely never use again. The XYL is happier, too, which is—believe me—always a big, big plus.

However, when someone chooses a hobby or pastime or to get serious about any other endeavor, and he or she then makes the decision to not invest a little time and effort into learning more about it, it boggles my mind.

Do not get me wrong. Because we become amateur radio operators does not mean we have to gain the equivalent knowledge of an electrical engineer. I do not intend to open up my transceiver and take it apart just so I can put it back together again and learn how it works. What I am saying is that we should all have more desire to learn about things in which we have interest. Why would we take the plunge and insist on asking somebody else to do it for us?

The same thing goes for many other things in life. My granddaughter, the light of my life, begged for that microscope for months. Why would she ask grandpop to do the most basic of adjustments for her? Would you take up golf and then ask the club pro to hit the difficult shots for you? I think some would if they could!

How many people refuse to learn anything about income taxes (too complicated, no time, bad at math), then either fill out the short form because it is easier or trust somebody else to do it for them, leaving money on the table? How many people blindly invest (do not understand financial stuff, do not have time, do not want to learn) their 401K contributions in only their company's stock and lose scads of money in the process? How many people have never taken the time to learn the basics of how an automobile works and then are shafted by unscrupulous mechanics?

I cannot change the brakes on my car. I do not know how. Again, I could buy a book, read the instructions, buy some tools, purchase a good jack, and change them, and I would then know how. I choose not to. But I know enough about the job to know if I am getting fleeced! And if I ever decide I want to do it, you can bet I will learn how to do it correctly.

I am no expert on Wall Street, but I know enough to keep my meager retirement nest egg properly invested and diversified so I do not get heartburn when the subprime mess dominates the headlines. I can read. I can comprehend. I have limited time, just like you, but I think it is important enough that I learn all I can about the subject.

I do not stand there, swaying back forth in the breeze, waiting for somebody else to do it for me. Or complain because nobody volunteers.

Maybe it is the lack of self-responsibility that seems to be so prevalent today. My generation was so conscious of protecting our kids from anything bad, making sure their precious self-esteem survived intact, and that they wanted for nothing that we raised a whole crop of, "I don't know how. Do it for me!"

Or we gave them the attitude of, "I don't want to learn a skill so I can make a living for my family. I can't learn. It is too much trouble. I'm too dumb. Pay me anyway, though. It is not my fault I won't learn."

I see examples of it in the forums on the popular ham radio sites. Bless 'em, they do have the gumption to ask, and that is a good thing. But the post usually runs something like, "I just passed my General and spent $10,000 on a rig and amp. What kind of antenna should I buy?"

There are enough curmudgeons out there that the first replies will not be all that friendly. No, they will be downright nasty. Eventually, though, someone with a true mentor's heart will ask some questions and provide the newbie with some valid info, pointing him in the right direction to learn more, politely inviting him to search the site's archives for the hundreds of other answers to the same question, urging him to invest some time and effort in some of the myriad sources for antenna knowledge.

With a little exertion, that newcomer will pick a good antenna and learn something about antennas in general in the process. He will likely never be an RF engineer, but he will enjoy the hobby more.

Sometimes the original poster comes back with a thank-you, and a report that he or she has invested in an antenna book, visited the W4RNL web site along with several others, and is busy soldering feed line to some wire. But too often, the follow-up post is, "What a bunch of rude SOBs! I just wanted you to tell me which antenna to buy. I don't know how to make one!"

Sigh.

As never before in the history of mankind, we are blessed with access to knowledge. I can read about any subject I can imagine…free, no waiting except for the page to refresh…and some subjects I could never have thought of, even if I had wanted to. I just found a site that links to a dozen different free, online Spanish courses. Want to learn about the sex life of the tsetse fly? It's there. Need a manual for a piece of gear that was discontinued in 1972? Odds are you can download the PDF. Do a Google search for "antennas" and stand back!

If you want to learn about something, you can. You just have to invest the time and energy.

Let me make it clear. It is okay to ask for help. That is one of the best and most lasting traditions of our hobby. Many of us take great pride in being able to help newcomers get a good start in amateur radio, just as our mentors patiently helped us, back when dinosaurs roamed the earth and Marconi and I were in the same pile-ups.

At the same time, the mentor often learns while teaching, too. It is absolutely true that the best way to learn is to teach.

It is a cliché, but like most clichés, it is one because it is so true. Give a man a fish and you feed him for a day. Teach that man to fish and you have fed him for the rest of his life. Of course, the caveat is that the guy has to want to learn to fish.

I have infinite patience with him if he does.

I have zero tolerance if he wants me to catch, clean, cook and spoon feed him that nice sea bass. Then complain because it was not prepared the way he likes it.

The saddest words I know: "I don't know how. Do it for me."

But maybe the most hopeful: "I don't know how. Would you help me learn?"

It is not required that you become an evangelist or recruiter for your hobby once you get your license and start enjoying it. I just happen to believe that, for a number of perfectly good reasons, we need to do so, therefore I tend to encourage such activity.

Think about what attracted you to learn more about amateur radio. There are likely plenty of others out there who would be hooked just as you were.

In the next chapter, I will talk a bit about my ideas for spreading the word. If you do not hear the call, no problem.

However, if you do, go forth! Spread the good news!

Chapter 22 -- Amateur Radio is Not for Everybody: a Primer for the Ham Evangelist

See if you agree with this statement: it is a good thing to promote our wonderful hobby to as many people as possible and do everything we can to continue to grow our ranks.

Hard to disagree with that one, isn't it? We love our hobby and want every man, woman and child to join in on the fun. At least most of us feel that way. Adding to our ranks brings new perspectives, new people for us to get to know, new interests to broaden the appeal of the hobby. It also helps justify all those valuable swatches of frequency spectrum that other services continue to eye greedily.

Come on in! The water's fine!

But hold on a second. Maybe a lyric from a Jimmy Buffet song is more appropriate: "The weather is here. Wish you were beautiful."

In addition to writing books and cluttering up the ham bands, until my retirement from my day job, I made money to support my hobby by working in marketing. And one of the first things marketers do is decide who our target is for whatever product it is that we will try to market to them.

Successful marketers do product development and design to meet the needs of a particular group of potential customers. Does the product already exist in some form? Is there competition? Can we differentiate ourselves enough to create demand? Can we manufacture it and distribute it at a price point where we'll make a profit? Do enough people want this product that we can sell sufficient units to make some money? Will it solve enough people's "problems" that it will be successful? Paint me a picture of our potential customer and convince me that he or she will want what we produce. Arrange to distribute that product in a way that it is readily available to that target group so they can buy it if they want to. Plan and purchase advertising so it efficiently reaches that target group with our message. Make certain that message is clear and differentiates us from the competitors. And make sure the message in that advertising is directly aimed at the potential customers for that product.

Finally, we marketers want to be sure we have a clear goal for what we want to accomplish. Is it to make [eople buy the product? Maybe, at least in the long run. But often that is not the primary action we seek. We might just want them to recognize our product on the shelf among all the other boxes. That's called brand awareness. Or we might want to inspire them to go to a web site and learn more. Or submit a form for a brochure. If they buy based on our message, fine, but everything we say and do—and all that money we spend—may be aimed at simply creating awareness. Then the customer can decide for himself if he wants to take the next step.

Find out what people want.

Give them what they want.

Tell them you are giving them what they want.

There it is. Marketing 101 in three short sentences!

Targeting. It sounds sort of sinister, calculating. But equate it to using a Yagi-type beam antenna. A vertical is a perfectly good HF antenna, but it pull in and sends out precious RF hurtling off in all directions equally. That multi-element Yagi concentrates the RF into one point on the compass, making it stronger and easier for the DX station to understand.

Of course, you have to know in which direction that DX station is and what sort of reply he likely expects. Aim so the station is off the side of the beam and, well, good luck! Send him a burst of PSK31 when he is expecting SSB and see if he responds to you.

Believe me, I am totally in favor of showing amateur radio to lots of people. Doing a special event station, inviting the public to Field Day, doing presentations at schools, retirement homes, civic clubs—all great ways to acquaint people with our hobby. Those sorts of efforts should be designed to impress interested folks among the crowd, inspiring them to learn more. It might also buy us a bit of sympathy if our station is klutzing up their TV picture or our antennas are not in congruence with their sense of acceptable landscaping.

In marketing, we call this "shotgunning." "Throw it against the wall and see what sticks." Like the vertical, it has some advantages, but it is not nearly as efficient as the Yagi in targeting our message.

How many people walking their puppy past your Field Day setup might coincidentally be interested in learning enough about electronics to get a ham license? If you crowbar your way into a Chamber of Commerce meeting, how many in the crowd are buying what you are selling? What if you set up that same type operation inside the local science museum? Or gave a talk about solar activity and propagation to the astronomy club at a local college? Or invited a storm-spotter group to observe your club's Simulated Emergency Test activities? Or allowed a high school Spanish class to talk with a station in Costa Rica?

Does your club have Power Point presentations aimed specifically at different groups? One for elementary school-aged kids with lots of whiz-bang (including Morse code...let a youngster hear his name in Morse and watch his or her face light up), one for high school kids with emphasis on computers, SDRs, ISS, Echolink and the like (show them an Altoids-tin QRP radio and the more technical-minded will be fascinated), and one for retirement or senior citizen groups with emphasis on creating friendships around the world, even if they are physically challenged.

Who would you think the most likely target would be to accept amateur radio and want to learn more? Kids? I think so.

Forget all that "they are only interested in cell phones and texting" noise. Make it cool and present it in a cool way and kids—some, not all—will get curious.

Teens? Every generation maintains the upcoming flock of young people is taking our civilization to hell in a handbasket. We have all mostly turned out pretty well, though. How many of you first got the radio bug in your teens? Even if you waited thirty years to do anything about it.

I rest my case.

Messaging. I'm not talking about the National Traffic System and your section CW net. I am talking about what you tell people that might cause them to do what you want them to do.

I maintain that none of us—you, me, your club, the ARRL—has the money, expertise, or time to sell ham radio as a hobby en masse to a wide, diverse audience. What we all can do is target an effective message to the proper audience in such a way that we can cause people to investigate us. Then they can decide if they want to join the club.

Our goal should be to entice some of them—the more the merrier—to get just enough of a whim that they will seek out information. It is actually much easier today, in my opinion. When I started, back when Lincoln was president, interest in amateur radio came mostly by word-of-mouth. If a local ham (W4OXU, now SK) had not started a class at the high school, I wonder if I would have ever pursued my interest in things radio. And turned it into a 22-year career in broadcasting which morphed into advertising and marketing.

Now, with the Internet, I can Google and Wiki and get the skinny with ease. Those who denigrate the ARRL for this or that should at least look at their offerings for would-be hams and make constructive comments. There are a bunch of materials on the League's web site if someone is interested including a great video that attempts to appeal to the new "maker" and "hacker" movement. Our hobby is a natural fit for the folks who pursue this type of activity and this video is a perfect example of what I mean about targeting and messaging.

I do think much of the League material hits the right notes: cutting-edge technology, emergency communications, radio-sport, worldwide friendships. Something in there should spark some interest in our most likely suspects if it is targeted at the right ones.

I submit that you have little hope of selling somebody completely on becoming a ham at Field Day or during a program at a civic club. Not unless they have been pretty much sold already. Instead, give enough information that those who are interested will go to the web, to the ARRL site, or your club web pages. (You do have a "Getting started in ham radio" page on the club site, don't you?)

Or maybe they will take you up on your invitation to come to a meeting where you will make them welcome. You will, won't you? Make them feel welcome, that is? Plant the seed. Target the message.

Do not, however, make them drink from a fire hose or scare them away with jargon and a bunch of inside stuff. This is not an initiation to test their commitment. It is a sales pitch, trying to convince them to learn more. Fan the spark! Do not douse it with too much info or by spending two hours arguing about the club by-laws.

Here is an idea: when presenting to high school groups, talk about technical careers. You think juniors and seniors in high school are not already thinking about what they will do for a living? Despite what you may hear, many of them—male and female—have a technical bent, too. Amateur radio is a great way to follow a technical hobby and prepare for a career as an engineer or scientist. Mention the Nobel Prize winner who is a ham and developed many of our digital modes. Talk about all the early computer innovators who just happened to be hams. Mention the astronauts on the International Space Station who routinely chat from orbit with hams back on the home planet. Have a copy of the editorial from the October 2010 issue of *CQ*

Magazine handy. It talks about previous recipients of the "Young Ham of the Year" award—an engineer who owns his own software consulting company, a physician at the Mayo Clinic, a Shakespearean actress. One recent winner is pursuing a degree at Georgia Tech in aerospace engineering and another is a software design engineer.

Who are we competing against for the attention of prospective new hams? Anything that captures the imagination of people is competition for amateur radio as a hobby. That and inertia—turning off *Dancing with the Stars*, getting off the couch, and learning enough basic electricity to pass a test.

What makes our hobby different? Worth the effort? What do we offer that people cannot find in other pastimes? Why should I spend my hard-earned money on a transceiver and a tower instead of on a ski boat or tennis lessons?

Show the wide range of interests that can be pursued in our hobby. Explore the possibilities of combining other hobbies and interests with ham radio. How about camping, RVing, radio-controlled models, history, stamp collecting, weather-watching?

I bet you can think of plenty more.

Action. What do we want that bright-eyed prospective ham to do? No article about spreading the gospel of amateur radio would be complete without mentioning mentoring. I know. As mentioned, I do not especially like the term "Elmer" either, and

I certainly would not use it when evangelizing about the hobby. But I am proud to be called an "Elmer." I love the spirit of it. I am delighted when I run into some of the people that I helped get started in the hobby and have them tell me how much they appreciate it.

If you see a twinkle in someone's eye during a presentation, or if a young person sticks around a little longer than his buddies when you operate from a Boy Scout camp, take advantage of that opportunity. Set the hook. You do not have to make him a ham that red-hot minute. But you can certainly say and do the right things to make him go home and Google "amateur radio." Or email you later and ask come by and watch you operate your station.

At the same time, do not make some of the mistakes I see being made all the time. Shave for a public event or a presentation. Wear deodorant. Dress comfortably but leave the antenna-erecting togs at home.

If you are an introvert, have someone there who is comfortable talking with strangers. Let guys who are better at public speaking do the presentations. Rely on Power Point but do not read the slides to the audience.

Have some toys there. Raising somebody across town on a two-meter FM repeater may not be all that impressive but to some, it might.

Do not be too technical. The electronics may be just what they are looking for, but it can send others screaming from the room.

Keep it upbeat, interesting. Have a stack of flyers, even if they are generic stuff downloaded from arrl.net. Add the club web site address even if you just write it in.

You may not realize it, but many people's perception of ham radio is that odd, funny-smelling uncle who hid out in the basement with all those noisy radios. Or the geek next door that comes in on the stereo. Do not confirm the stereotype!

One final suggestion: if we want to attract people to our hobby, we need to be more welcoming. There. I said it.

Whether it is at club meetings, on the air, or in posts on forums or web sites, consider that would-be amateurs are judging our ranks by what they see, hear and read. I'll give you a quick example.

In a recent discussion forum, someone with a 2-by-1 call sign commented on the CW capabilities of a new transceiver recently put on the market. Someone else—and I will resist calling him a jerk, though that was exactly what he was—chastised the poster mightily, and even included a copy/paste from the FCC database that indicated that the 2-by-1 fellow was a relatively new ham who passed the Extra exam without benefit of having passed a code test. Basically, he told the fellow he had no right to talk about CW since he was a no-code Extra, and, for that reason, he would never be "a real ham."

I believe strongly in freedom of speech, and discussion forums are intended to allow people to express their opinions. However, had I been someone considering pursuing the hobby and I saw such tripe, I might reconsider whether I really wanted to attempt to join this particular curmudgeonly fraternity.

You get my point. We have a hobby that almost sells itself, but it is not for everyone. Besides, nowadays it has more competition than ever before. That means we need to target a strong message at the right prospective amateurs. Show them enough of what the hobby has to offer and that will convince those with a true interest to consider learning more. Then be there to show them more, not chase them off.

If we do these things, we will get the new, young blood into our hobby that will keep it vibrant and alive for all of us.

If we do not, it just will not be as much fun as it could be.

Chapter 23 -- My Top Ten Suggestions for Newly Licensed Amateurs

I do not for a second pretend to know it all. I doubt if I even know a smidgen, a word my dad used that apparently means itsy-bitsy. But after more than fifty years in this fascinating hobby, I think I have picked up a few things by osmosis. Much of that came from other amateurs who took the time and effort to give me the benefit of their experience, sometimes calmly and patiently, sometimes not so politely or diplomatically. For some reason, we call those folks "Elmers," though I have already made the case for using the term "mentor" when approaching those who may not understand such an archaic-sounding term.

In the spirit of those mentors—and as a way of thanking them—I would like to offer ten suggestions I would make to any new amateur radio op out there who might stumble upon this book. I truly believe that if you will take this advice, you will get more from the hobby.

Now, I am not so egotistical as to think I have the secret to eternal happiness in Hamdom, or that I have all the answers. And, for that reason, here is my first suggestion:

Listen! Listen before you get your license and after. I know you are itching to key that microphone or slap that key, but listen to how the other guys do it. Sure, you will hear some operators doing things that others may not think are correct. You may even hear some things that will curl your hair. There are goofballs in any hobby.

In general, though, you will quickly get a good idea of procedure, accepted behavior, and standard protocol. Hopefully, you will notice people speak English so you will know to limit the jargon. Some actually have interesting things to say.

You will also notice very little usage of terms and practices that you may have experienced if you previously operated on the Citizens Band frequencies. Remember that the FCC originally took an amateur radio band away in order to create that very specialized service. Some ill will lingers. Additionally, many see CB as a bunch of ham wannabes who either do not have the will or intelligence to pass the exam.

I do not agree and believe CB radio has been a pathway for many to enter into ham radio. Just understand that there may be some irrational prejudice against you if you came from CB. Then, if you persist in using slang and operating practice that may have been just fine on 11 meters, you are only making it easier for those nuts to pick on you.

When you think you have a pretty good idea of how to do things on the amateur radio bands, join right in. Most amateurs welcome new ops. Especially when they don't yell, "Contact! Contact!" and ask for everybody's "first personal."

That brings me to my second suggestion for the newbie to ham radio:

Talk! I can tell you about many who worked hard to get their licenses, only to hesitate once they were finally bona fide. They could never bring themselves to push the microphone button or try their hand at that Morse code key.

Shy? Maybe. Scared. Almost certainly. All of us were when we made that first over-the-air contact. My hand was shaking so that I could hardly pound out the characters on my old J-38 straight key when I had that first QSO.

Let me assure you, though, that there are many, many fine folks out there anxious to talk with you and learn more about you. I believe you will be surprised how excited that person on the other end of the contact will be to learn he or she is your first contact. As with any group of people, there will be some who are more interested in hearing themselves talk than in getting to know you. On the other hand, most of us got into the hobby because we enjoyed meeting and learning more about people, their lives, their locations, and more.

Let me also urge you to have something to say. When you run out of something to say or feel the conversation is dragging, take polite leave and look for someone else while allowing the other fellow to do the same thing.

Start with the signal report, of course. And your name. Not "handle" or "personal." Name. Spell it phonetically if it is difficult to understand. Do not be too cute. "My name is Bill…'Boy, I love ladies.' Bill." Or: "Bob…'Bottles of beer.'" Quite often the other station has already pulled you up by call sign on the computer and knows your name. But if it is "Charles" and you prefer "Chuck," tell him.

Then you can tell the other station about your rig and antenna. I suppose the weather is still fair game for chatting. But then move on to other more interesting things about yourself, unless you are in the midst of a blizzard or broke the record for high temperature in your city that day. What do you do for a living or what are you most interested in at school? What got you interested in the hobby? What do you think will be your favorite aspects of ham radio? What other hobbies or pastimes do you pursue? Use the old salesman's trick: find common ground. You will be surprised how often you and a ham operator across the country (or world) have something in common that leads to a very pleasant chat.

Make notes about what the other person says and comment on them. In short, carry on a conversation, just as you would if you were sitting in the park on a bench next to your new friend.

If he needs or wants to move on, he will tell you so. Do not be offended if he ends the QSO with you and then promptly calls CQ and starts up another one with someone else. That is the way it is done, and is no slight to you.

A big part of our hobby is communicating. So communicate!

Learn! Maybe you are perfectly happy once you pass the exam to forget what little you learned about electronics and communications. That is fine. Many enter the hobby for other reasons than building radios and designing antennas and being able to read a Smith chart in their sleep. (Smith chart. There is something you may want to learn about already!)

However, I would urge you to maintain a healthy curiosity about those technical aspects of the hobby. The reason? It will enhance your enjoyment of the things you really do like to do.

Example: you got your license because you like the challenge of talking to lots of countries around the world, or to try to win contests—what we call "radio-sport." You will be much more likely to enjoy DXing or contesting if you understand a bit about antennas and how they work. Or how to hook up a computer to your radio for rig control and keeping your contest log. Or how to tweak your SSB audio so you can cut through the clutter to work that rare DX station or run up a big score in Sweepstakes.

What happens if you have a glitch during a big contest weekend? You may be able to do a simple repair or workaround if you understand how your rig functions.

Maybe it was the opportunity to assist with weather spotting and emergency communications that got you hooked. Knowing how radios work and how signals propagate can be handy if you are handling communication from a disaster scene and have a problem. Or in planning for a community service event.

In addition to all that, science has shown us time and again that we postpone many of the effects of aging by continuing to use our brains as we grow older. It is like exercising a muscle! Continuing to learn, being curious about how this stuff works, can actually keep you young.

Who among you wants to argue with trying to stay young?

Four: Ignore the curmudgeons! Speaking of old-timers and being argumentative, let me warn you about a certain segment of our hobby. Oh, you would find similar impolite duds if you pursued stamp collecting or quilting or fly-fishing. These are the goofballs who resent anyone else trying to get into their protected little tribe. Often that is because they fear newcomers will attempt to change something they think is perfect already and the one thing they fear most is change. Or they resent people who—they believe—got into the fraternity without having to go through the same hazing as they once did.

You will absolutely hear hams decry the loss of Morse code as a requirement for getting a license. Most have gotten over that one, but some never will. The fact that you had no choice when you took the test is lost on them completely. And never mind that CW operation has actually gone way up since it was no longer required that new hams learn the code.

You will hear others moan and cuss and claim the exam today is so easy it should come in a box of Cracker Jack. Why, way back when they took the test, you had to know some electronics. Today's hams can memorize the answers and do not know squat.

That is part of the hazing that the curmudgeons feel should be a part of the process. To keep out the riff-raff, they say. Never mind that by far the most and worst rule-breakers— according to no less an authority than the Federal Communications Commission—are older hams.

Again, these are mostly people who are either naturally prejudiced against anybody who is not like them—young, vibrant, smart, active, new—or simply fear change of any kind. Do not allow your feeling to be hurt when—not if—you run across one of these ignorant killjoys. As mentioned already, their presence in our hobby is in about the same proportion as the number of them in the population in general.

Besides, the biggest knob on most radios is the one that allows you to easily change frequencies and to listen and talk elsewhere.

Move beyond the two-meter HT! Okay, this just happens to be one of my pet peeves. As near as I can tell, a majority of people entering our hobby do the same thing once they pass the license test. They buy themselves a two-meter FM handie-talkie.

Why not? They are relatively inexpensive, the antenna comes already hooked up and a part of the radio, and as soon as your new call sign shows up in the FCC database, you can have your batteries charged and begin making contacts through the local repeater. You are on the air with a little, bitty handheld radio!

Trouble is, those radios usually come with a "rubber duckie" antenna, which may make the radio very compact and easy to take with you, but it is a notoriously inefficient radiator of RF energy. So you purchase a quarter-wave whip and screw it on, making the radio tend to tump over when you set it down and you poke yourself in the eye a lot, but you do seem to be able to be heard on the repeater a bit more.

Still, it is a struggle. You try to use the little thing when you are in the car and get nothing but gripes from guys who try to talk to you. You are setting up a shack in the basement but you cannot even hear the dang repeater down there, much less talk to anybody. See, you are still only running five watts or so. And VHF is a line-of-sight part of the spectrum. If you cannot see the repeater antenna, it will be difficult having that antenna pick up your puny little signal.

There is nothing wrong with buying and using an HT. They are handy, easy to take with you, and can, in the right circumstances, provide you good, solid communications. Just be aware of the limitations. I use one most days when I take my morning walk. I can get into several local repeaters and it makes the exercise much more bearable to be able to listen and talk. But I know where on my typical route I will have trouble with which particular "machines." (We tend to call repeater stations "machines." Do not ask me why.)

I am simply urging you not to judge the amateur radio experience on how it goes with that little HT. Even with millions of dollars invested in cellular telephone infrastructure, you still get dropped calls and lots of grief using your cell phone, right? That little device is really little more than an HT but with much more sophisticated and elaborate "machines" out there to make them work. And still, they often fail to do satisfactorily.

Here is an idea. Plunk a magnet-mount quarter-wave two-meter antenna on the roof of your car and hook your beloved HT to that. It will make all the difference in the world. Better still, invest in a true mobile two-meter radio that runs thirty or forty watts. Get one for the house, too, with some kind of outdoor antenna.

And quickly move to other bands and more aspects of the hobby, too. That conveniently brings me to the next suggestion for you new guys:

Avoid getting into a rut! It is easy to do. You find one facet of any hobby that you really enjoy and you do not explore anything else. You fish in the same lakes for the same kind of fish all the time. You collect the same stuff over and over. Before you know it, you are bored with the whole thing.

Same with ham radio. You love chasing DX stations, working new countries, trying to get the certificates for getting a hundred of them confirmed on five bands. Great! I love chasing DX, too.

But sometimes the bands are not cooperative. I have already worked and confirmed stations in all the countries that are riding in that day on the wind. Okay, I will just shut off the radio—though I had planned to spend all morning down there in the shack—and go watch TV or something. Working those same countries over and over. Boring!

Then, before you realize it, it has been weeks since you even turned on the rig.

Wait! There are plenty more things you can do in the hobby that may even slip up on you and become your favorite thing to do. For a while. Until you discover a new favorite thing to do. And you are never bored.

Try futzing around in a contest. Move to a different band or mode. Give digital a try. Be on the lookout for some of the special operations such as IOTA (Islands on the Air), SOTA (Summits on the Air), county hunting, or special event stations. Build a kit or try a new antenna. Write an article for one of the web sites. Venture outside the ham bands and do some SWLing (shortwave listening). Use Google and find nets that might be dedicated to another one of your interests.

Wow! That is a perfect segue to my next suggestion.

Combine your hobby with another interest! Do not tell me you have no other interests besides ham radio. Of course you do!

One of the wonderful things about our hobby is that it can be easily included as a part of so many other popular activities.

Do you fly model airplanes or have an interest in starting to? They are typically "RC." Radio controlled.

Are you a boater or sailor? A rig in the boat only adds to the pleasure, and could even be valuable in case of an emergency. There are several nets devoted to hams who have rigs in their watercraft, too.

Camping or RVing? Ham radio is a natural fit. Many, many hams have stations installed in their RVs or take along low-power radios and compact antennas so they can enjoy listening or communicating from wherever their travels take them.

Hiking or more basic camping? I hear many hams each weekend, operating from some mountaintop or wilderness area, using QRP and a simple antenna. They are, however, literally working the world from some truly wonderful spots.

Those are only a few examples but I think you get the idea. Here is one more suggestion along the same lines. When you do combine your ham radio hobby with other pursuits, tell other hams about it. Or tell fellow hikers or boaters or stamp collectors how great your radio hobby meshes with what they do.

Join a club! I know. Some of us are just not "joiners." After a hard day at work, we hate to climb back into the car and drive downtown again for a club meeting. Then there are those clubs who seem to resent anyone new from diluting the perfect little organization they have built. Or they spend two hours of a two-hour meeting arguing about the club's bylaws and officer elections and never get around to talking about radio.

Those kinds of clubs exist. On the other hand, there are many, many vibrant and exciting organizations out there who will welcome you heartily and will make that drive back downtown well worth it. Once you know the other members, you will know who to go to in order to get questions answered. You may be surprised to learn that they will volunteer to come help you hang an antenna or hook up a digital interface. They may sponsor special event stations, organize communications for community events, participate as a group in contests, and put on a heck of good time at the ARRL Field Day event each year.

The club may put on a hamfest or swap meet, too. You might want to help or just get first dibs on all that gear for sale.

Of course, they probably sponsor license classes so you can more easily upgrade to the next class. Oh, and learn some new stuff, too. Speaking of learning, many clubs give great programs on a variety of subjects related to the hobby, and that could also allow you to see other sides of ham radio that you had not yet considered.

At its basics, though, a good club fulfills a need we all have: to belong to a tribe, a group of people who have the same interests as we do. There is something satisfying about being around folks who speak the same language and have pursued the same pastime as you have.

Even if you do not join a local club, I will vociferously urge you to become a member of the American Radio Relay League. By your membership, you are making our national organization stronger and better able to protect our interests and frequencies, and to expand the scope of the hobby. You also get a great magazine, *QST*, and many more benefits that make the dues a wonderful investment.

Becoming a club member—local or ARRL—also presents you with a platform to follow my next bit of advice.

Give back to the hobby! One of the truly magical things about amateur radio is how so many of its followers freely give back time, money, expertise and support to the hobby. Here are just a few ideas that occur to me. You should be able to think of many more.

Instead of selling an old piece of gear cheap or hauling it to the dump, loan it to a new ham so he can get on the air or get more enjoyment out of the hobby. If you write well, do articles for the hobby web sites about an experience you have had or something you have built. Offer to do a program at the club on that same topic. Help teach a license class. Get certified as a Volunteer Examiner so you can assist in administering exams. Support the ARRL by joining and give money to the spectrum defense effort and other worthwhile causes.

There is one very big way you can give back to the hobby in which you have found so much fulfillment and enjoyment. That is my tenth suggestion for the newly-licensed amateur radio op.

Become a ham radio evangelist! Now that you are licensed and have begun to see all that the hobby has to offer, you become a true evangelist for ham radio. Set up a station in the park on a Saturday and be ready to answer questions from passers-by. Be prepared to tout the hobby and your local club if someone spots your amateur radio license plate and asks what it is all about. Refer questioners to the club web site (if it is well done and helpful to newcomers) and to the ARRL web site. Invite friends and relatives to your shack and show them your setup. Let them hear some QSOs in progress and even send a little Morse code if you are proficient. If you do not already, you will soon know which frequencies you should NOT allow them to hear!

Be a mentor! Once you are comfortable doing so, offer to help someone interested in joining our ranks, or assist a new ham in getting on the air, making that first contact, or upgrading to a higher class license. Few things are more rewarding than seeing someone you helped get started go on to enjoy the hobby as much as you do. Or more!

Take an HT to school or work, if permitted to do so, and explain to your classmates or co-workers what it is and how it can be used in disaster situations. And just for fun, too.

It is true that some still think of hams as that old guy, secluded in his basement, causing interference to everybody's TV on the block. Others still consider us to be nerds, or electronics nuts, with little or no social life. Still others do not know the difference between amateur radio and CB and think we are the guys in the Trans-Am and big-rig truck, rescuing Sally Field from Jackie Gleason.

You have the opportunity to set them straight. Tell them what we really do and what the hobby is about in the twenty-first century. Be ready to answer those challenges I mentioned in my introduction. Some believe we have lost our relevance and, in the day of the smart phone and Facebook, there is no reason for amateur wireless as a hobby.

Not true! We are more relevant than ever, and we still have the opportunity to lead in development and implementation of tomorrow's technology. Plus we just plain have fun doing what we do.

One of the greatest ways you can help the hobby to grow and attract other bright minds is by being an evangelist for the hobby. There is another benefit.

It will also increase your own enjoyment as you learn more, too.

Chapter 24 -- The Roundtable

Nobody really remembers when the group first started meeting, heating up the band with their conversation, jokes and carryings-on. A couple of guys began chatting most evenings just below 3900 on the 75-meter amateur radio band. Others dropped by when they could—some of them long-time friends of the first conversationalists, others total strangers who just joined in to give an opinion or ask a question or get a signal report—and over the years, hams came and went. The roundtable mostly grew, regardless the status of the sunspots or changes in the hobby or whatever else was going on in the world.

The topics were all over the spectrum, though politics and religion were mostly avoided. So were medical conditions unless one of the members was having particularly threatening issues or had a funny story to tell about his gall bladder. Some went SK ("Silent key" or passed away). Some went inactive. Others moved to other bands or modes, drifted back in every once in a while, or simply faded away, not to be heard from again.

But for years, the group's regulars still showed up most evenings, anywhere from just-after-supper to late, late, late. Weekends and holidays, the roundtable sometimes carried over into the wee hours of the next day. Some nights there were only a pair or three stations. Some nights there were a couple dozen.

And stations checked in from Colorado to Florida, Canada to New Mexico. Summers were slowest with all the crunching of the QRN (static). Sometimes it was tough when the band "went long" in the winter evenings, but sometimes European stations or ops from the Caribbean or South America hopped aboard and contributed. No matter, the nightly roundtable carried on, an almost unstoppable force.

It was informal and friendly. If someone got out of line, he was gently chastised. Jammers and tuner-uppers occasionally did their thing but everyone learned early that if these disturbed individuals were totally ignored, they always moved on. Everyone understood that those guys did what they did for attention. When they got none, they went elsewhere in search of it.

Joe from St. Louis and Claude from Louisville were the informal heads of the group. They had good stations, power with great antennas, and their central locations were handy when the band went squirrelly. They were both natural storytellers, too, with senses of humor that seemed to make the transition from audio to RF and back to audio just fine.

But there really was no "net control." Any time there were more than a few stations, the group dispensed with the formal rotation and just went to a conversational "speak up" format, like a group of friends gathered on somebody's deck, having a chat. Some nights, when everybody identified their stations at the same time, it sounded like an odd chorus singing a strange, discordant tune, with even the cricket chirps of a few CW identifiers mixed in.

The topic one particular night centered—as it often did—on antennas. Joe was talking about his latest addition to the antenna farm, a skywire horizontal loop, 260 feet of copper wire strung from tree limb to tree limb in his backyard. Someone had just asked him what kind of antenna seeds he had planted to grow such a monstrosity when a new and very tentative voice edged in amidst all the noise on the band.

"That's a great antenna, very quiet on receive . Uh...hi, fellas. This is K4NSD."

"Well, good evening, K4NSD. 'Never Say Die!' Welcome in. I don't think we've had the pleasure before, and you know by coming into this group, you immediately bring doubt and suspicion about your sanity, right? Just doing my duty and giving fair warning."

"Thanks, Joe. Uh...well...I feel like I know all you guys. I've been lurking out here for a long time now tonight is the first time I've piped up."

"Glad you came in," Claude chimed in. "What's the name and location?"

"It's Tommy. I'm in Nashville. The truth is, I'm a new ham. I just got my license a couple of months ago and you guys are my first contacts here on HF."

There was a burst of congratulations and welcomes and "what took you so long to key that mike?" from the assembled group of amateur radio operators, chiming in from ten different states.

"Well, I had to build up my nerve, you know!" Tommy said with a chuckle. "Took me a while to get up an antenna, too, and I went with the skywire loop, mostly based on what I heard you guys talking about here every night."

"Well, Tommy, I hope we haven't led you astray in other areas!" one of the other members kidded. "If I had known you were lurking out there, I might've convinced you to do an extended double zep..."

And the antenna conversation was off and running again, the default topic of conversation for the next few minutes or the next few hours.

From that evening on, K4NSD became a regular member of the group and was soon one of the favorites. For the first month or so, he brought mostly questions, but then he was offering constructive advice on his own. It was clear from his comments that he was studying, learning, growing in the hobby. He sometimes brought back stories of DX exploits on other bands, not bragging but sharing. Or word of how he had been of help on the Maritime Mobile Net on 20 meters to a sailboat having some issues down in the Gulf of Mexico. Or an anecdote about something that happened on one of the mobile-operator-assist nets on 40 meters.

Tommy was a good storyteller, a good listener (as most good storytellers are), and he was soon regarded as one of the roundtable's anchors, relatively new ham radio operator or not.

Finally one night, curiosity got the best of one of the other regular nightly participants. He opened his mic and asked the question that was likely on the minds of others in the loose network.

"Tommy, I don't remember you ever telling us what you do for a living," the op noted. "We're usually real nosy about such things, and you seem to have a lot more ham radio time than most of us guys out there who are working forty hours a week so we can pay most of it to Uncle Sam."

There was an abnormally long pause, a few bursts of static, a distant heterodyne somewhere up the band a ways.

"Aw, I work from home," Tommy finally answered. "I take lots of breaks and seems like the radio just draws me to it. Y'all can identify with that, I bet. This ham radio is addictive, in case you haven't noticed! By the way, I've been thinking about a vertical for 40 meters and I was wondering your thoughts on how many radials would be the best if I..."

Several months later, somebody noticed K4NSD had not checked in for a few nights. That was unusual. And the group had come to enjoy his stories and encouragement. Tommy always offered good conversation, excellent insight, and a keen sense of humor that had long since made him one of the favorites of the bunch. He was missed when he didn't join in.

On Sunday night, there he was, though, chipper as ever, with news about an article he had tracked down on the Internet about balun design.

"Tommy, we missed you the last few days," Claude told him. "We were afraid you had stuck your hand in the high voltage on that amplifier of yours or something equally tragic."

"Not even a newbie like me would do something that dumb, Claude," Tommy responded with a laugh. "I had to be out of town for a few days. No big deal."

And that was that.

Then, six months or so later, another one of the group regulars, Bill, who lived in Western Kentucky, had an announcement for the bunch.

"Guys, we are driving down to Mobile to take a cruise, and I was thinking we'd stop along the way to eye-ball a couple of you so-and-sos. Even though that might completely destroy the lofty image I have of some of you once I see how ugly you are in real life. But at least it would give you a chance to see how handsome and well-preserved I am for a man of my advanced age. Tommy, we'll be coming right through Nashville and I'd love to stop in, visit for a few minutes, and buy you a glass of sweet tea."

The band was filled with static crashes, a bit of splatter from somebody down the band giving his compressor a good workout. Then Tommy finally piped up.

"When did you say you all were coming through?" he asked. Bill told him the date. There was another short pause. "Aw, heck! I've...uh...got to be out of town that day. All day long."

"Well, how about on the way back through? That'll be Sunday, the 11th, if we don't get hijacked by pirates or I decide to run off with one of those beautiful bikini gals down in Cancun."

Yet another pause. Nobody said anything to fill the gap. They waited for Tommy's answer.

"Man, Bill, I'm missing meeting you every which way. I've got some business stuff going on that day that will tie me up all day."

"Can't you see he's avoiding you, Bill?" Claude opined. "I've met you in person and I don't blame the boy one bit."

"He sure is, coming up with work on Sunday," Bill kidded. "I'm about to get my feelings hurt and you all know how danged sensitive I am."

"I'm sorry, Bill," K4NSD jumped in quickly, his voice far more serious than the other ham's had been. "You know that I'd love to meet you, and I really am partial to sweet iced tea, and especially when somebody else is buying. Let's make it for sure the very next time you come through. By the way, you taking a radio with you on the cruise? You thought about trying to do something from the cruise ship or at least mobile down there and...?"

This time, everybody on the group that night noticed how quickly and obviously Tommy changed the subject. But then the topics flowed, K4NSD was his usual great raconteur, and before long, they were wrapped up in the QSO—mostly led by K4NSD—and they thought no more about it.

Tommy always seemed to have something to add to the conversation, regardless the theme of the evening. Especially interesting were his recounting of QSOs with his friends across the country and around the world on the other bands. Before long, most members of the 80-meter roundtable felt they knew Charles in Vancouver, Will, the sheep rancher in New Zealand, and Barney, the antique-car collector and avid DXer from Wales just as well as Tommy did, all based on his descriptions of them and recounting of their chats.

One of the guys brought up Tommy's employment again after K4NSD told of a three-hour chat he had had earlier that afternoon. It had been with an interesting fellow who lived thirty miles north of Moscow and whose father had fought against Hitler in World War II.

"Tommy, I'd like to know how you keep from getting fired," one of the roundtable members remarked. "I spend three hours doing anything but putting together cars on an assembly line, my boss sends me packing."

A rare, long silence again. Only a bit of splatter swirled around in the ever-present QRN.

Then Tommy responded with his usual booming signal and smooth audio.

"Remember, I'm...uh...self-employed. That means I have an idiot for a boss and a fool for an employee!"

Several guffaws cracked open VOXes and the chat turned toward jobs, bosses, and employees.

Then Tommy was not on the roundtable for a week during in mid- August. Some speculated he might be on vacation, though he had not mentioned such a thing. Others wondered if he had rig or antenna trouble, though he certainly seemed to have the technical knowledge by then to fix most any fixable problem. As always, he was missed. Frankly, the net seemed to drag a bit nowadays without his spark.

When he failed to join in for the eighth straight night, Joe and Claude exchanged emails. They were making plans to drive down to the Huntsville, Alabama, hamfest the following weekend.

They had already decided to meet up in Nashville and ride on down the rest of the way together.

"If he doesn't show up in the meantime, let's plan on dropping by Tommy's QTH and checking on our buddy," Claude wrote. Neither admitted it but part of the reason would be simple curiosity. As much as Tommy brought to the group, there was still a maddening sense of mystery about the guy.

The QRZ.com web site confirmed the FCC database address. There were no photos or information about K4NSD on the QRZ.com page, just a note that his call sign had been searched over 20,000 times. Google Maps showed his QTH to be in a neighborhood south of town, only a few blocks off Interstate 65.

It was mid-day on Friday when Claude and Joe met at a Cracker Barrel restaurant and enjoyed lunch together. The two of them had only had an "eyeball QSO"—seen each other in person—three or four times over the years in which they had been chatting with each other on the nightly roundtable.

After lunch, they took Joe's car and drove into Tommy's neighborhood, easily locating the house number on his mailbox out front. A customized passenger van sat in the driveway. The Tennessee amateur radio license plate proclaimed it belonged to "K4NSD."

Only a couple of hams would have noticed the arc of ladder line feed line spiraling out of a tree in the backyard and toward the rear of the house.

"Bingo!" Claude proclaimed. "We have successfully tracked down the highly mysterious so-and-so!"

It never occurred to either man that Tommy might not have wanted to be found, that their visit might, instead, be considered an intrusion. They thought of Tommy as an old friend, and though they had never seen him face-to-face, it was exactly as if they had had coffee with him practically every day for the past ten years, chatting across the table in person.

An older lady cracked the door open cautiously when they rang the bell.

"Yes? May I help you?"

"Good afternoon, ma'am," Joe said, removing his call sign ball cap. "We're a couple of buddies of Tommy's, Joe and Claude. We're passing through town and just wanted to stop by and say 'hello' to him."

She studied them warily for a moment.

"We're ham radio operators," Claude added. "Amateur radio buddies."

The door opened a bit wider and the woman smiled.

"Oh! Excuse me and my bad manners. You never know these days. Tell me your names and call signs and wait right here and I'll check to see if...I'll be right back."

The two men looked at each other, but before they could wonder too long, the lady was back, opening the door for them, smiling as she warmly invited them inside. She led them through a neat living room and down a short hallway into what would typically be a den or family room. The smell of cookies permeated the air. The lady did not wait for them to ask.

"You gentlemen go on in and I'll get you some fresh-baked cookies, just coming out of the oven. And which would you like, milk, coffee or iced tea?"

They thanked her and placed their orders.

The big room was dark, the blinds closed against the afternoon sun, but they could hear the sound of a SSB conversation coming from a speaker somewhere. And, as their eyes adjusted from the brightness outside, the dial of a radio came into focus. But strangely, it appeared to be suspended from the ceiling on chains and cocked at an odd angle, not resting on a desk or in a rack.

Then they could see a man, lying beneath a sheet on a big hospital bed. He was amazingly pale, his arms white, resting at his sides. He turned his eyes toward the visitors but his head did not move. A microphone hovered on a boom near his pillow, inches from his dry lips.

"C'mon in, guys," the thin man said, his voice weak but still very, very familiar. He did not offer a hand. "Pardon me if I don't get up and shake your hands. I know. This is what happens when you wrap a motorcycle around a telephone pole. The telephone pole wins every single time."

"Gosh, Tommy, we had no idea," Claude said, stunned.

"I know. I know. I really never saw the need to burden you guys with my little problems. I was seventeen, invincible, going much too fast and some grandpa pulled out in front of me. Mom, I can't believe you let these two old crooks into our home! Call the law! Quick!"

The last was directed at the lady who was already setting down a plate with several cookies stacked up on it. And though there was no smile on Tommy's lips, there certainly was one in his expressive eyes.

"Sit down, fellows, if you have a few minutes to visit. Now that you've tracked me down, I'll show you my setup."

There was an elaborate bunch of spaghetti-like tubes within reach of his lips that he could use to blow into in order to control band-switching, mode selection and other parameters on his radio.

"Mom has to come help me if I need to change bands quickly to chase DX or something," he told them. "I used to do some CW, using some kind of gizmo the rehab folks rigged up and some of the local hams helped me install. It was a touch-screen kind of thing...tied to glasses that let me focus...on a key so I could blow into the tube...and send a character."

Tommy paused then, out of breath, as if the words he spoke had drained him completely of all energy.

"Man, that's amazing!" Joe said, and he was sincere. "Quite a setup."

"Look, Tom, we didn't mean to barge in," Claude told him. "We just had no idea..."

"No idea at all," Joe added. "It's amazing what you have done...getting your ticket, getting on the air, being such a great member of the roundtable. Being such a good operator, even though..."

"I've gotten a lot more...out of that bunch...than I'll ever be able to contribute," Tommy said, and again those few words seemed to claim what was left of his breath.

The two visitors eased down into chairs, took a cookie each from the plate, and accepted the offered glasses of cold iced tea from Tommy's mother.

"We just wanted to make sure everything was all right so we decided..."

"Aw, I appreciate it, guys. I've been...over in Memphis...the hospital over

there...kidneys...darn things are acting up...lately. Just got back...this morning...the trip kind of wore me out."

Unlike the roundtable when Tommy was aboard, the other two hams carried most of the conversation. Tommy seemed to feel better after a while, seemed to forget how hard it was for him to breathe. For a bit, it might just as well have been the three of them, chatting away on lower sideband just below 3900 on 75 meters. Even Tommy's voice was beginning to sound near the same as it did there on the shortwaves.

Finally, after three cookies and three big glasses of tea and a good hour of the in-person roundtable, Joe stood up and put his hand on top of Tommy's still one.

"Buddy, it has been great visiting with you, but we got to get on down to Huntsville. We have to get checked into our room in time for the DX dinner tonight. Is there anything we can help you with before we get out of your way?"

Tommy asked them to tighten the speaker connection on the back of the rig. It had gotten flaky lately and cut out when his mom moved his bed to make it up. And he had them crank up the transmit audio gain and compression on the radio just a notch.

"My voice gets a tad weak sometimes lately," he explained, but asked them to let him know next time he was on the air if he was splattering or distorting with the new settings. He worried about such things. Always had.

"We'll be back home Sunday and maybe you'll feel like...get a chance to get on the roundtable with us," Joe told him.

"I plan on it. And you can tell me what gear you saw at the hamfest. What they had good on the tables in the boneyard." The two visitors started for the door. "Oh, and guys. Thank you. Thank you for letting a new ham break into the group that night. And for being so nice and helpful...to a newcomer...who thought Ohm's Law was a cop show on TV."

"Hate to tell you, old man, but we do that for everybody, not just K4NSD!" Claude said with a laugh. "We'll put a band scope on that audio Sunday and see how it works. Now me and Joe have to get on down the way and see what prizes we are going to win and then have to load up and lug back home."

Tommy blinked hard and there was the slightest twitch of his cheeks that could have been the beginnings of a smile.

"Seventy-threes, guys. You'll never know...how much I appreciate you."

"Seventy-threes, Tommy," Joe shot back with a wink.

Both men were uncharacteristically quiet on the ride down I-65 that afternoon.

They hurried home on Sunday and had their rigs on and tuned up early for the roundtable, waiting to hear their friend when he checked in. There were a good dozen stations aboard that evening, and the subject matter ranged far and wide, from the things they saw and heard at the big hamfest, to the later-than-usual sporadic-E activity on six meters, to the beginning of college football practice at several stations' favorite schools, all of whom were certainly going to win the national championship that year.

Later on, somebody asked Joe and Claude about their stop in Nashville, about meeting Tommy. The two let everyone in the group know his situation. They did not figure he would mind. Not so long as they did it the right way.

Then they were back on the subject of propagation, the new QRP radio kit Joe bought that day, the boat anchor amplifier Claude purchased and made Joe help him haul all the way out to the car, both in Huntsville and then again when they got back to Claude's car in Nashville.

"That's all right," Claude added. "I toted that QRP kit for him for a while, too. That thing must've weighed two or three ounces! I'll be sore for a week."

But though most of the group lingered later than usual for a night before a work day, there was no K4NSD aboard that evening.

Nor did he show up on Monday or Tuesday night either.

Wednesday evening, about an hour after the first of the crew showed up, a W4 station broke in, a station nobody recognized, but with a good, smooth, strong signal. Joe quickly acknowledged him and told him to come on in "and put your feet up and stay a while. We can use a signal like yours to scare the riff raff away."

"Thanks for letting me in, guys. My name's Cliff and I'm in Franklin, Tennessee, just south of Nashville. I just wanted to...well...I'm afraid I have bad news. Tommy Fowler, K4NSD, passed away Monday morning."

For several seconds the 75-meter band went about as quiet as anyone had ever heard it. Even the static and scratching of distant signals up the band went silent.

Claude was the first to speak up.

"Gosh, Cliff, that is some tough news," he said, his voice breaking slightly. "We really appreciate you coming onboard tonight to tell us, though."

"There's one other thing I wanted to share," the W4 said. "I know Tommy would want me to tell you this. Especially you guys. I think you, of all people, will understand it." Cliff's voice trembled slightly as he spoke. If it was possible to hear someone swallow hard over the air and from hundreds of miles away, then everybody on the roundtable that night heard Cliff swallow hard. Then, back in control, he went on. "This is something Tommy told a bunch of us one day when we were over at his place helping put up an antenna or something. He asked us to sit down for a minute. That he wanted to say something. He told us, 'Boys, from the day I first transmitted a signal on the air, from the night I broke into that roundtable on 75 meters, I ceased to be paralyzed anymore. The day those guys welcomed me into their group, I was no longer tied to this bed and that feeding tube and all these catheters. I traveled the world starting that night on the roundtable, and along the way, I met the most amazing people. That bunch...you guys who help me stay on the air...the friends I have made all over the planet...all of that gave me my legs and hands back and made it possible for me to live with this thing.'"

    This time it sounded as if somebody had let the air out of the band. Even the QRN, the splatter, and the squalling heterodynes chose to remain hushed for a few moments.

    The group talked about Tommy for a while, and would do so off and on for weeks. Nobody would ever replace their friend, they decided.

    Then, with Cliff sticking around and joining in, the topics that night drifted back to the usual: who they had seen at the hamfest the previous weekend, what the latest piece of gear reviewed in *QST* was, whether sending iambic CW was worth the learning. They almost half-expected to hear Tommy jump in and defend a point.

Then, during a short lull just before ten o'clock, a young, high-pitched voice suddenly chimed in, interrupting the flow of the group, and tentatively saying, "Uh...breaker, breaker."

"Sounds like we have someone who has dared to break into this bunch of wool-gatherers," Joe responded. "Well, welcome, breaker. Come on in and tell us your call sign, your name and where you are."

"Uh...this is...uh...K M 5 C Q P." The youngster said the number and letters slowly, as if he was reading them off a slip of paper. My name...handle...uh...personal...is Danny Smith and I'm in Little Rock, Arkansas."

"Well, Danny, welcome to the roundtable. It's our pleasure to have you with us tonight. We are delighted to have Little Rock represented. Can we do anything in particular for you or do you just want to come on in and raise the average IQ of this bunch by twenty or thirty points?"

"Yes sir. See, I just got my antenna up in the attic..." The signal faded deeply and then came back. The audio carried a bit of distortion. The youngster's voice trembled slightly. "...signal report, if you don't mind, sir. I just got my license last week and...well...you are my first contact on the ham."

There was a short pause before Joe and then Claude and then each of the other stations came back in turn. They would not only give Danny his signal report but enthusiastically welcome him to amateur radio, 75 meters, and the nightly roundtable.

In that short pause, it was easy to sense the big grins on the faces of each and every ham radio operator who was listening in to the roundtable just below 3900 on the 75-meter amateur radio band.

(This chapter was inspired by Ric Sims K4SCI and Mike Ferguson KE4UMD, both now "silent keys.")

ABOUT THE AUTHOR

Don Keith is an award-winning broadcaster, a best-selling author, and has been a licensed amateur radio operator since 1961. He was first licensed as WN4BDW in 1961, earned his General class license later that year, and then became an Amateur Extra class licensee in the mid-1970s, receiving the call sign N4KC.

He was twice named *Billboard Magazine*'s "Broadcast Personality of the Year," won every major broadcast journalism award in his state from the Associated Press and United Press International, and was an on-air personality, journalist, station owner, program director, and manager in a career that spanned over two decades.

Don published his first novel, *The Forever Season*, in 1995. It has remained in print continuously since and was named "Fiction of the Year" by the Alabama Library Association. His 24 other published works, fiction and non-fiction, cover such topics as NASCAR racing, broadcasting, college sports, submarines, and World War II history.

Don lives in Indian Springs, Alabama, with his wife, Charlene, has three grown children, and two grandchildren. He operates all the shortwave amateur radio bands as well as VHF and uses most modes, including CW, SSB, PSK31 and FM. He enjoys DXing, contesting, antenna experimenting, and just plain rag-chewing.